Lady Georgiana Charlotte Leveson-Gower Fullerton

Laurentia

A Tale of Japan

Lady Georgiana Charlotte Leveson-Gower Fullerton

Laurentia
A Tale of Japan

ISBN/EAN: 9783741130182

Manufactured in Europe, USA, Canada, Australia, Japa

Cover: Foto ©Andreas Hilbeck / pixelio.de

Manufactured and distributed by brebook publishing software (www.brebook.com)

Lady Georgiana Charlotte Leveson-Gower Fullerton

Laurentia

LAURENTIA:

A Tale of Japan.

BY

LADY GEORGIANA FULLERTON.

BALTIMORE:
KELLY & PIET,
Printers and Publishers,
174 BALTIMORE STREET.
1866.

CONTENTS.

CHAPTER.		PAGE.
I.	THE ARTIST'S HOME,	1
II.	STRUGGLE AND VICTORY,	16
III.	GRACE UCONDONO,	35
IV.	A VISIT TO THE PALACE,	53
V.	THE EVE OF THE FESTIVAL,	78
VI.	THE JAPANESE BRIDES,	93
VII.	A CONVERSION,	109
VIII.	A BAPTISM,	132
IX.	PERSECUTION,	146
X.	PREPARATION,	158
XI.	MISGIVINGS,	173
XII.	THE TWO MATTHIASES,	186
XIII.	MARTYRDOM,	201

PREFACE.

The incidents embodied in the following little tale, though for the most part founded on fact, are not related with strict regard to historical accuracy, or to the chronological order in which they took place. It has been attempted to give a picture of the Church of Japan in the sixteenth century, and to illustrate in the shape of a narrative the peculiar character of the Japanese converts to Christianity, rather than to compose a regular historical tale. But it may be safely asserted that not one trait of heroism, not one act of self-sacrifice, not one sentiment of exalted virtue from the lips of priest or catechumen, woman or child, which finds place in these pages, but has its counterpart in the annals of a Church founded by a saint, fruitful in the most remarkable virtues, and which, after a hundred years' duration, did not die away from the decline of faith or the lukewarmness of its members, but was suddenly extinguished as it were in a sea of blood, leaving behind it glorious records of its existence, but not one priest to carry on the service of religion, and but very few Christians to perpetuate its memory.

The character of the Japanese race is marked by peculiar features, which probably told on the destinies of the Church in a country which its historian, Father Charlevoix, calls the England of Asia. There was a strength of will, an independence of spirit, a dogged attachment to existing institutions in that people which has no parallel amongst the nations of the East. The resistance of the unbelieving portion of its inhabitants to the establishment of the Christian religion was as desperate as the efforts of the converts for its propagation were strenuous. The heroic courage of the Japanese Christians, their readiness, or rather eagerness, to renounce their worldly possessions, to suffer torments and death itself for the sake of their religion; the audacity with which they braved the anger of their heathen Sovereigns, and with which even young children asserted their faith in the face of their alarmed and indignant parents, are in some degree traceable to the influence of natural character, and hardly perhaps as strong evidences of the power of Christianity over their souls as the generosity with which they embraced the less dazzling virtues of obedience, humility and evangelical poverty, singularly opposed as they were to their previous habits, feelings, and tone of mind.

The Jesuit fathers were often obliged to restrain their impetuosity, and check their ardor for martyrdom, by representing to them that, although the sacrifice of their lives was no doubt in one sense a gain to themselves, at the same time they were not justified in endangering the safety and

the very existence of the Church in their native
land by too rash an onslaught on the prejudices
of their countrymen. Through a long period of
years they had succeeded in guiding the destinies
of that Church through the many perils which
had beset it. It had been often persecuted, often
driven from one province to another; some of its
converts martyred, and others banished; but it
had still maintained its ground and a firm hold
on the hearts of its children. But at the period
in which the scene of this little story is laid many
circumstances were combining to precipitate the
course of events which finally led to the massacre
of the Christians and the apparently total annihi-
lation of Christianity in Japan. The impetuous
character of the Japanese converts, the jealous
susceptibilities of their rulers; the vainglorious
boastings of a Spanish naval officer, reported in
an evil hour to a proud and irritable monarch;
the national feeling roused to alarm by the dread
of foreign domination—all these causes together
were sowing seeds of destruction in as fair a field
as had ever been cultivated by evangelical laborers or watered by the blood of pious martyrs.
But may we not indulge the hope that in that extraordinary country, which, for two hundred
years, has refused admission to Europeans, and
excluded from its shores her travelers, her traders
and her priests, traces may yet remain of the true
religion which had taken such deep root in its
soil, which so many thousands of its inhabitants

had embraced with a zeal and devotedness which has no parallel except in the first ages of the Church; that when the civilization of our days, with all its attendant train of evils and advantages, forces its way, as soon as it must, into Japan, and opens the door to Catholic missionaries, letting in the light where the will of an energetic and spirited people has so long maintained darkness—that their teaching will yet find a response in the dim reminiscences of former days; that possibly in some few favored spots, in some out-of-the way corners of the land, from father to son, some portions of the faith may have been handed down, and some few Christian practices maintained.

May God grant this reward to those who toiled and bled in the days of St. Francis Xavier and his successors; to the holy martyrs of the Church of Japan, and to those who, with patient prayers and ardent desires, are even now watching for the moment when Christians may once more tread that consecrated ground and preach the Gospel there, even if it be, as in the days of old, at the risk of their lives.

LAURENTIA;

A Story of Japan in the Sixteenth Century.

CHAPTER I.

THE ARTIST'S HOME.

The setting sun had just ceased to gild with its last rays the domes, the palaces, and the towers of Meaco, the capital of Japan, the residence of the Dairi, or Ecclesiastical Emperor, and of the Kumbo-Sama, the temporal sovereign of that ancient kingdom. As the moon rose in the dark blue eastern sky, the eyes of many worshippers turned towards it in that strange land where a strong religious instinct seems inherent in the souls of men, and, in the absence of the true faith, displays itself in almost every erroneous form of worship to which the corrupt tendencies of men's hearts, and the excesses of their imaginations, have at different times given birth. Towards the north of the town, enclosed within a triple range of walls, stood the palace of the great human idol of the Kamisian superstition—the awful, but helpless, Dairi—the representative of that hereditary line of patriarchal monarchs, once the supreme governors of the Empire; the framers of its laws and the absolute rulers of its destinies, but now set aside in idle and solemn state; superseded by the Kumbo-Samas, a race of wily and energetic statesmen and warriors, who gradually assumed the functions, whilst they left to their chiefs the bare semblance of authority —the homage of the multitude and the vain pomp attendant on their half-religious, half-nominal sovereignty.

In the streets which surround this abode, a death-like stillness reigns; no profane footsteps may venture to tread, uninvited, the sacred precincts; but outside these strictly guarded walls an incessant activity prevails. Clouds of dust, raised by the traffic of a populous city, obscure the air, and the ear is deafened by the vociferations of its six hundred thousand inhabitants, all engaged in the various pursuits of commerce, industry, and pleasure. From the neighboring mountains three great rivers descend and feed the broad-bosomed lakes, the ever-flowing fountains, the numberless diverging rills, which fertilize the wide and otherwise barren plain, in the centre of which Meaco sits like a crowned queen, with her encircling amphitheatre of hills, and her diadem of temples: five hundred splendid fanes, gleaming like jewels through the deep verdure of the pine and cypress groves.

At the same hour, in one of the most retired streets of the city, a maiden of about twenty years of age was sitting at work in the front chamber of a small but exquisitely neat building, adorned according to the fashion of the country, both within and without, with paintings, inscriptions, and devices of various sorts. Every window was ornamented with flower-pots, as is always the case in the houses of Japan, but in this instance more than ordinary good taste was evinced in the choice and arrangement of the miniature shrubs and various colored blossoms which filled the graceful white porcelain vases, enwreathed with China roses, and encircled with green leaves. The folding screens which divided the apartments of this little abode were covered with graceful scrolls, and pictures of birds and flowers. Moral and religious sentences, drawn from the Holy Scriptures, and from the maxims of Confucius, were likewise inscribed over the doors, or painted on the walls. Numerous articles of beautiful workmanship lying on the floor, in an unfinished condition, seemed to indicate that this was the residence of an artist of no ordinary abilities. Fans there were of so fragile a texture, so elaborately carved, and so admirably colored, that they seemed to emulate Nature's handiwork in the delicate tracery of the fern or the mimosa, or the soft blending of her hues in the geranium or the heart's-ease. Sculptured beasts and birds, whose life-like forms and attitudes might have deceived their prototypes of the groves and of the plain, were standing about waiting for the finishing touch of the master's hand.

To the maiden belonged the humbler task of making and fastening to the handles of the fans which her brother painted the silken or gilded tassels which each required. She knew how to vary their forms and colors with fairy-like ingenuity. Her own appearance was in keeping with her pretty abode and her graceful occupation. If there was nothing peculiarly costly in her dress, if the number of her flowing robes fell short of that which the fine ladies of Meaco habitually wore, they were so becomingly put on, the yellow texture of her skirt was so beautifully embroidered, the pattern of her flowing vest harmonized so well with the red girdle which encircled her waist and the coral comb which fastened her dark hair, that a painter, of the Ventian school, could scarcely have found a fitter subject for the display of brilliancy and harmony of coloring, than the workshop of the Japanese artist and the figure of his sister seated in the midst of her silken skeins, and engaged in her laborious though apparently fanciful avocations.

She was wistfully gazing at her slender store of gold and silver thread, and holding up one of the fans in a discontented attitude, when her brother Matthias entered the room.

"Still at work over those fans!" exclaimed the young man, whose slender form and hectic coloring betokened delicate health, or at least a fragile organization. "Why truly, Laurentia, you spend more time about the tassels than the fans themselves are worth."

"It is the fault of my dear old friend the blind pedlar. He promised to bring me this week a large supply of gold thread from Nangazaqui, but he has not kept his word. I hope no evil has befallen Matthew. I do not know how I should get on without him. From my earliest childhood I have been used to look forward to his visits."

"There are strange rumors afloat," answered her brother; "the Kumbo-Sama is reported to have used strong language about the Christians. The ladies of Omura refuse to listen to his emissaries, and the blame is laid on the fathers. People say that his anger is beginning to rise against them as the black clouds gather round the heights of Saxuma when a storm is at hand. Will it be prudent for you to go to the palace, Laurentia? Who knows but you may be questioned as to your faith? At all events, you had better not take with you *these* fans," he said, pointing to a row of highly finished ones which were ornamented with Christain devices or paintings of a religious character.

Laurentia shrugged her shoulders. "As if the Empress did not know that I was a Christian! As if, begging your pardon, brother, that was not her very reason for wishing to see our fans. At least, I greatly suspect so. Her messenger said that the Empress understood that you had painted one for the King Bartholomew, which he always carries about with him, and that if you had a similar one at home I was to be sure and bring it with me, as her Majesty had expressed some curiosity to see it. I would not for the world miss this opportunity of entering the palace. Who can tell what the result may be? Old Matthew assured me, some time ago, that the Empress had a secret desire to embrace the Christian faith."

"But why not wait till the Kumbo-Sama's wrath has cooled down a little? Why not go another day?"

"Another day! when I am expected to-day!"

"You might feign sickness."

"Feign! Is it to a Japanese maiden—to your own sister—that you speak of feigning? After all, the worst that could happen to me would be to die."

"What words are these, Laurentia?" cried a well-known voice at the door, and the old pedlar stood by the maiden's side, unstrapping his heavy box and wiping his forehead; "do not speak of dying when there is so much work for a Christian maiden to do in this poor country of ours. We shall all die when God chooses, and if the Kumbo-Sama gives us a helping hand to heaven, by cutting off our heads, he will be sure to get many a Christain's blessing. To live, to work, and to suffer, is often far harder than to die." Matthias kindly led the old man to a mat, and begged him to sit down and rest his weary limbs.

Matthew, the pedlar, was one of St. Francis Xavier's converts, and ever since the day when he had been baptized by the Apostle of the Indies, the burning charity which had consumed that great man's heart seemed to have kindled in his own a kindred flame. He had not changed his mode of life. He remained a poor man travelling from place to place, selling his wares, going about from the palace to the cottage, from the crowded sea-port to the secluded hamlet, doing good, praying without ceasing, preaching the Gospel, in his quiet way, to the rich and to the poor, to the learned and to the ignorant. Often scoffed at, often repulsed —for he was poor, and his countrymen despised poverty; and he was unlearned, and they worshipped learning—but still making his way into many a heart, and enlightening many minds, through those very means which God has appointed for the conquest of the powers of this world; the very same through which the devils had to be driven out of old, even in our Lord's own day; fasting and prayer; the apostolate of voluntary suffering joined to holiness of life. It is the same story over and over again. The fishermen and the tent-maker walking on foot into Imperial Rome; the merchant's son at Assisi renouncing his heritage and hooted at as a madman; the warrior-saint, the high-souled nobleman, Ignatius, pointed at as a beggar in the streets of Paris; St. Francis Xavier dying alone on the shores of a foreign land, all illustrate the same moral, all tell the same tale—

Satan on the one hand wielding against the souls of men his weapons—riches and honor—and Christ vanquishing him through the strength of poverty, the might of humiliation.

"Have you found means to see the Empress yet?" Matthew inquired, as he felt among his wares for the parcel from Nangazaqui which Laurentia was expecting.

"This very evening I am going to the palace," she eagerly replied. "Her Majesty has expressed a wish to see the fans Matthias paints, and particularly the one the fathers ordered as a present for King Bartholomew. He has since made several of the same kind. The holy name of Jesus is in the centre, in letters of blue, scarlet, and gold. Above it is a crown of thorns, and beneath it the three nails, and other emblems of the Passion. Then there is this one also, with a copy of the picture which hangs over the altar of our church—the divine Infant and His blessed Mother. Father Rodriguez, the Kumbo-Sama's interpreter, says that when the King of Omura saw it, he was so ravished with its beauty that he stood like one transfixed, and in that very hour resolved to become a Christian. Oh, dear Matthew, would that you could see it!"

The old man smiled, and lifted up his sightless orbs to heaven. His mind, so long given to contemplation, and ever haunting as it did the midnight cave of Bethlehem, and the home of Nazareth, had doubtless often pictured to him the Babe and His immaculate Mother in sweeter and loftier beauty than the hand of Raphael or Correggio ever depicted them on glowing canvas or frescoed walls.

"And then, this picture of the Crucifixion," she continued, "it is so beautiful. But do you think I can venture upon showing it to the Empress? The cross, the crowning glory of our faith, is a stumbling-block to unbelievers. What will she think of our Lord dying like the vilest malefactors?"

"You who have been so long a catechist," said her brother, "should know how far you can venture to unfold the truths of religion to the uninitiated. Now you are about to have the Kumbo-Sama's wife for a catechumen, discretion must be your guide."

"Well, I suppose discretion is a virtue, but it is not one I love; I like courage better."

"Take care, young maiden," said Matthew, "that you do not make courage into an idol. The fathers say, it is one that many a Japanese worships in his heart even while he destroys the visible ones in his house."

"True," answered Laurentia, "we are brought up to depise death, and abhor cowardice; but death on the field of battle, or in the presence of the Kumbo's officers of state, who respectfully leave it to a man to execute his sentence on himself, is far different from the lingering tortures to which the Christians have been ere now subjected. Nothing but the firm hope of immortality, and the aid of divine grace, could nerve the soul to meet with joy and calmness such agonies as those."

"I suppose there is nothing which one man has borne that another cannot endure," said Matthias; "and yet men are so differently constituted! What is exquisite suffering to one person is scarcely any pain to another. However, if it is the grace of God which supports the martyrs, it signifies little, I suppose, what their physical peculiarities may be."

There was something tremulous in the voice of her brother, which struck painfully on Laurentia's ear. She looked up anxiously into his face, and saw that his pale cheek was flushed. The hectic hue died away in a moment, and left the deadly paleness behind it. He, however, answered with a smile her inquiring glance. Reassured, she turned again to the pedlar, and said—

"Have you travelled to any great distance, Matthew, since we last saw you? Have you made any new converts? Is it true, what we have been told, that a great lord, in the Ximo, heard you speak of the only true God to his attendants, and was so struck with your words that he exclaimed, 'If a poor pedlar can thus discourse about his religion, what must the bonzes of that religion be!' and that he went at once to the fathers at Nangazaqui, and was instructed and baptized?"

"It is true; and the Church received that day a noble heart into its fold. God ordains wisdom out of the mouth of the old and the weak, even as out of that of babes and sucklings. Little children are often apostles, and the old man sinking into his grave can also sometimes act an angel's part. I have never opened my box in the street or on the road side, and heard the sound of approaching footsteps, that I have not asked our Blessed Lady and God's dear servant, Father Francis, who baptized me, to speak to the hearts of those who stood round me. Then words sometimes rise to my lips which astonish me. They seem to teach the poor sinner who utters them as if they were not his own. And then these little pictures, they have been apostles too in their silent way. I passed through a village in the mountains some months ago where Father Francis had once been and made several converts. No priest had ever found his way there again. They had his abridgment of the Scriptures and a little print of Jesus and His Mother. He had taught them the Creed, the Our Father, and the Hail Mary; baptized thirteen of them, and appointed an old man to be their teacher. He had died, but they never let go the faith Father Francis brought them. They said their prayers, and patiently waited for another messenger from God."

"Oh, have they a priest now?" exclaimed at once the brother and sister.

"A brother from Ozaca is gone to instruct them, and one of the fathers will soon join him."

"Matthew, if a great persecution should arise, you will certainly be put to death as a teacher of Christianity."

A divine expression passed over the old man's face when Laurentia said these words. Not the enthusiasm which gleamed on the maiden's brow—something more deep, more humble, more holy than enthusiasm. "That would be too good for me," he gently said, and felt in his box for a rosary, which he gave to Laurentia.

"I will wear it round my neck to-night, when I go to the palace."

"Do not act so madly, Laurentia!" exclaimed her brother. "You are running risks enough by going there at all. Be persuaded, sister, and only take with you the fans painted with birds and with flowers; you can show the others another time to the Empress."

"Do you think then that my object is to show off your paintings, and to sell perhaps a dozen fans? If that were my sole purpose, I should not indeed take so much trouble." Matthias left the room with a dark cloud upon his brow, and the sound of his retreating footsteps was heard on the paved alley of the little garden.

"Maiden," said the old pedlar, as his quick ear detected the sigh which escaped her, "have you thought enough that those who would win souls to Christ must begin by fighting another battle?"

"With their own passions, you mean—I know it, I feel it—I have often shed tears, and done penance for the faults of my temper, and now I have sinned again, and the peace of my heart is gone." She passionately exclaimed, "Oh, how can I speak of

Christ to-night to those who know Him not, when I, who know Him, have offended Him? No blessing will rest upon me, for the stain of sin is on my soul. What shall I do?"

"Kneel down and say to God what you have said to me—say it meekly and lovingly, and doubt not that He will bless you. One moment of loving sorrow sets us right with Him—He can then clasp us to His sacred heart and entirely forgive us—He can trust us with His highest gifts, and employ us in His service."

"O Matthew, would that I heard often such words as these! Would that our fathers were always with us to teach, to absolve, and to direct us! If we could worship the true God with perfect freedom I should not then so passionately long to die—to have done with this world. But it is with fear and trembling that we enjoy these dearest blessings. Though at this moment we have the servants of God with us here in Meaco, we are daily threatened with their banishment. Each time we go to church we feel it may be the last time we see or hear them. Oh, it is a weary struggle! Would that we lived in Nangazaqui, the Christian city."

"We must dwell where our lot is cast, and where each of us has an appointed work to do, maiden. And now, farewell. My poor prayers will follow thee to-night. I know thy courage will not fail. I know thy faith and thy hopes; but I will remind thee before I go of what Father de Torres, the

successor of Father Francis, once said to me when
I was going blindly to work, like a blind beggar
that I am."

"Do not call yourself a beggar, Matthew," indignantly exclaimed Laurentia; "you are not, you
never were a beggar—no beggar ever sat by
my side, in my own house, as you are now doing."

"There is a beggar called Lazarus, the fathers
tell us, who sits in Abraham's bosom. If you had
shut your door upon him, Laurentia, you might
have fared badly in the next world. Thank God,
you have shown kindness to one who is indeed a
beggar for Christ's sake. It will be very good for
you to have done so when you go to your account."
The maiden listened meekly to the old man's rebuke, and gently reminded him that he had not
told her what Father de Torres had said.

"Well, he bade me recollect that in the Litany,
which we repeat every day, we call the Divine
Mother the prudent as well as the powerful Virgin,
and that in this country we must not risk the lives
of our fellow-Christians and the welfare of religion
for the sake of following our rash impulses and
setting others at defiance."

"I will bear in mind this lesson," said Laurentia, with a bright smile, which Matthew felt,
though he could not see it beaming upon him,
"and when my too eager heart beats wildly in my
breast, I will say, *Virgo prudentissima, ora pro
me.*"

The pedlar shouldered his pack, and directed

his steps towards the College of the Jesuits, whilst Laurentia, with her black and gold casket in her hand, and shrouded by the long veil which the Christian women in Japan always wore out of doors, proceeded through the crowded streets to the palace of the Kumbo-Sama.

CHAPTER II.

STRUGGLE AND VICTORY.

FATHER ORGANTIN, the superior of the College of the Jesuits at Meaco, was seated at a table covered with various books and manuscripts, occupied with the translation of some religious work into the Japanese language, when one of the lay brothers knocked at the door and told him that a messenger had arrived in great haste from the Fortress of Tagacuqui, and that Justo Ucondono, the worthy son of Tacoyama, one of the first Christians of Japan, and the Governor of that stronghold, entreated the father instantly to come to him.

Father Organtin desired that the messenger should be shown in, and after the customary salutations had taken place, the latter proceeded to urge, with all the eloquence he could command, the importance of the message he was entrusted with.

"Is the noble Justo ill?" the father anxiously inquired.

"Not in body, but in mind," was the answer. "His soul is ill at ease, and, to judge by my master's haggard looks and agitated manner, he greatly needs your spiritual advice and assistance."

"No one in this country has a better right to command my services," the father replied with some emotion, "but at this moment my leaving Meaco is all but an impossibility. The Kumbo-Sama is much irritated against the Christians, and an imperial edict, sending us into banishment, hourly expected. How can I leave at such a time my community and my flock?"

"Father," exclaimed the envoy in an impressive manner, "Justo Ucondono is one of your children, and he is on the brink of despair."

"He is indeed my dear son, and hitherto one of God's most faithful servants. He has never feared death in His cause. What strange circumstance can have so deeply moved his noble heart? Speak the truth, my son, the whole truth, for your words make me painfully anxious."

"I cannot reveal to you, reverend father, for indeed I know not the cause of my master's anguish. Messengers have come to Tagacuqui from the east and from the west, and held long parleys with our chief. Some of the neighboring sovereigns have visited him, and in the last instance an envoy from the Kumbo-Sama brought him a letter in his Imperial Majesty's own writing. I have seen a bed of flowers blighted in one night by the winter's first frost; it was bright and beautiful the day before, and the next morning it had become a heap of black disfigured weeds. I have seen the fair promise of a beautiful harvest, in the smiling fields of Ozuma, in a moment destroyed by the tornado. I have seen a town, in the Corea, the picture of wealth and prosperity when the sun rose upon it, before noon turned into a mass of ruins through the shock of an earthquake; but never have my eyes witnessed so sad and sudden a change as I beheld in my master's face when he called me to his side, after that last interview, and delivered to me the paper which I now place in your revered hands."

Father Organtin took the missive from the kneeling messenger, and read the following words: "To none but you can I impart the dreadful situation in which I am placed. I dare not trust its details to paper, and cannot act without your advice. Come to me my father, and save your son Justo from crime or from despair."

"I cannot resist such an appeal," exclaimed the father; "at all risks I must go to him;" and, starting to his feet, he called the lay brother who had ushered in the messenger, and ordered him to get a horse instantly saddled. He then gave some brief directions to those whom he left in charge of the College, and was just preparing to depart, when Father Rodriguez, the priest who acted as interpreter at the court of the Kumbo-Sama, arrived in haste, and communicated to his superior the imperial commands, that he should immediately repair to the palace, to confer with the Sovereign on matters of life and death.

It required all the self-command acquired by the long discipline of years to enable Father Organtin calmly to endure the delay thus offered to his journey. But the pious servant of God had been too long accustomed to subdue every merely human impulse, and to act continually under the influence of supernatural motives, not to submit his own will without hesitation to the will of his Divine Lord. He turned his horse's head from the road to Tagacuqui to the one which led to the palace with the same outward tranquility, the same inward acquiescence, as if his soul had not been intensely longing to hasten to the side of his afflicted son in Christ.

This holy man was still in the prime of life, though the toils, the austerities, and the labors of many years of missionary work had tinged his hair with grey, and made him look older than he really was. The lines in which Johnson describes the warrior King of Sweden might have been applied in a far higher sense to this veteran soldier of the Church of Christ:—

> "A frame of adamant, a soul of fire;
> No dangers fright him, and no labors tire."

There was a power in his eye which few could withstand, and men who had never known what fear was had been seen to quail before its glance, whilst its kind, benignant expression could at times melt into tenderness the most hardened sinner. As he stood that day in the presence of the Kumbo-Sama there was an awful dignity about the Christian priest which awed for a moment the despotic monarch into forbearance. He had been but now burning with rage, but the serenity of that majestic countenance seemed to cast a spell upon his fury. His words were measured; he spoke of his respect for the missionaries, his high opinion of the stranger fathers, whose virtues and talents he admired, whereas he despised the hypocritical and dissolute bonzes, the native priests of Japan. He said that he had reposed great trust in his Christian subjects; that he had relied on their fidelity, but that now he found his confidence had been misplaced and his trust abused. Raising his voice, and his cheeks flushed with anger, he continued: "Yes, the wisest and most gifted of my vassal princes, the most valiant in arms, the most prudent in counsel, has dared to fly in my face, has refused to obey his lawful sovereign, and yield up to him the fortress he holds, immediately indeed from Fondasadono, one of the six rebel kings now in arms against the state, but which belongs, by every right divine and human, to the emperor, from whom both originally held it, and to whom he has sworn faithful allegiance."

"Has a Christian chief acted thus?" inquired the father, whose heart sank within him with a heavy sense of coming sorrow.

"Ay, your model Christians; your pious heroes. Tacoyama and his son Justo Ucondono disobey my orders; refuse to surrender the fortress of Tagacuqui, the key of my dominions; and when I sent troops to compel them to submission, they repulsed them by force, and closed the gates against them. The spirit of Vatodono still lives in his nephew. Justo, with a handful of men, and in such a fortress as Tagacuqui, can hold out for months against my army. But by all the gods of my country, by the divinities of Japan, which the Kumbo-Sama never invokes in vain, I swear, that unless he yields me that obedience which he owes me, and to which I have a right, every Christian in my dominions shall perish; every priest shall be crucified, every Christian church burnt to the ground, and the last trace of your foreign worship for ever effaced from this land."

The passion of the heathen despot rose into fury as he spoke, like the raging of the sea, which seems to increase in violence as it breaks on the firm motionless rock:—"Speak, father," he roared out; "speak! Your life, and the life of every Christian, is at stake. There is no possible escape for a single soul of your people, if your power— that power which men say is so great over the minds of others—compels not Justo Ucondono to submit. Go to him; go to him instantly, and use that wonderful influence you are thought to possess; that is, if you do not wish instantly to die with all your flock."

"Sire," answered the father, "it matters little to me, or to the Christians of this land, whether we die by your orders to-day, or to-morrow, or of old age some few years hence. God of these stones can raise up children to Himself, and from smouldering ashes and buried ruins new churches may spring up. To men who believe in one only true

God and a life to come, there is little to care for in the threats of the most powerful sovereigns. You can destroy the body, Sire; you are powerless against the soul; but there is a fear which can always move us, a danger which deeply afflicts us, that is, the fear that a Christian should commit sin; the danger that he may transgress God's commandments. Justo Ucondono has, I know it, sworn allegiance to your government, and done homage to you for his lands. Heaven forbid that he should take part with your enemies, and join in this unhappy rebellion. I will indeed go to him, as your Majesty desires—not to plead your cause, Sire, not the cause of your Christian subjects, for they are accustomed to suffer, and do not fear to die—but the cause of his own soul, for which I would willingly lay down my life."

"Plead as you will, and on what grounds you choose," replied the Emperor; "I know well that you are not afraid to die, though you refuse to kill yourselves—the only noble and dignified mode of dying in our opinion—but it is well known that you revel in tortures and exult in the Cross."

A bright gleam shot through the calm expressive eyes of the father as those last words were uttered. He gently bowed his head in token of assent, and then took leave of the Sovereign with as much composure as if the fate of the Church of Japan, the lives of his brethren, of his children in the faith, and his own, had not been trembling in the scale.

During the journey from Meaco to the fortress

of Tagacuqui, the feudal residence of Justo Ucondono, Father Organtin kept revolving in his mind all the circumstances connected with the past life of that just man, and vainly trying to account for the line of conduct he was now so inconsistently pursuing. His father, Tacoyama, had been one of the earliest converts of St. Francis Xavier, had carefully educated him in the Christian religion, had given him an invariable example of devotedness to the interests of the Church, of fidelity to her teaching in times of persecution, as well as of those domestic virtues which made the converts of Japan so conspicuous amidst their generous and high-spirited, but licentious and proud, countrymen. Justo's life had been a holy and consistent one ; the gifts with which nature had richly endowed him—beauty of features and strength of limb, a commanding intellect, a generous heart, and great abilities both as a warrior and a statesman—had all been held by him as talents to be used in the service of his Maker. "Man was created to praise, to show reverence, and to serve God, and in so doing to save his soul." That sentence, which contains in a few words a whole world of theological knowledge and sound instruction, had been familiar to him from the days when he had lisped it at the feet of the successor of the Apostle of the Indies. He had been trained in that spirit of detachment which is the true liberty of the soul ; and with the consistency between faith and practice which is a gift usually vouchsafed to an infant Church nursed by persecution and strengthened by sufferings, he had ever acted up to the teaching he had received, and held fortune, influence, existence itself, as possessions he was at any moment prepared to resign. His masters, in the spiritual life, had been sometimes obliged to check the ardor with which he was disposed to snatch at the crown of martyrdom, or to abandon, without a struggle, his property in order to lead in the deserts the kind of life through which St. John the Baptist, and our Lord Himself, passed on their way to the dungeon of Herod and the heights of Calvary. Father Organtin called to mind the bright smile with which the Japanese hero was wont to enter his cell and say, "Good news, father, good news; the bonzes are raging like their chief, because their time is short; the sword of persecution is about to be unsheathed; we may all be in heaven, please God, before the sun sets this day." And was it Justo Ucondono who was now standing on the verge of crime, on the brink of despair? It seemed almost incredible, and yet Father Organtin had seen many an instance which might make a man tremble for the noblest spirits, for the most fervent souls, and exclaim in the words of Scripture, "How are the mighty fallen!"

To behold again a face which we revere and love, to stand once more in the presence of one who has been to us for years as God's angel keeping guard over our souls, when a great anguish or a great misgiving has come upon us, is almost more than a breaking heart can bear. It was a strange meeting between those two men, united by an affection "passing the love of woman," and dreading to look upon each other : the one fearing to read the consciousness of guilt in a face where truth and goodness had ever been written as with a sunbeam ; the other, who had never yet known what it was to tremble, trembling in the presence of him who held, he felt it, his fate in his hands.

"My son," was all that Father Organtin could say as he noticed the wild look of Justo's fiery eyes unmoistened by a single tear.

A groan escaped the chieftain's quivering lips, and then he uttered these words in a low hoarse voice, "Cain said his 'punishment was greater than he could bear ;' my trial, father, is heavier than I can endure."

"My dear, dear son," said the father gently, "there is no intolerable trial to one who loves our dear Lord as you do. What can have moved you so deeply? Oh, my son, what enemy has done this ?"

Justo turned his almost livid face towards Father Organtin and answered :—"Are you aware, father, that you are speaking to a man who must be the murderer of his own children, or else doom to death all the Christians, men, women, and children, priests and people, in this land ?"

Father Organtin shuddered, but by a strong effort maintained his calmness. "How can this be ?" he added, in as firm a voice as he could command.

"My children, my eldest daughter Grace and my son Francis, are in the hands of the King of Arima. Before I had received any intimation of the intended rebellion against the Kumbo-Sama, I was induced to permit them to visit his court. My daughter and the young Queen had been friends for some time past, and she hoped to instruct her in the Christian faith, and win her soul to Christ. Now the six kings who have risen in arms insist on retaining my children as hostages. They claim possession of this fortress, and have sworn to put them to death if I surrender it into the hands of the Kumbo-Sama."

"Ah," said Father Organtin, "I heard that you had repulsed your Sovereign's troops and defied his authority. I understand now your sufferings; but I see no reason for despair."

"You turn pale, father, and yet you have heard but one-half of my dreadful story. Yesterday I had come to a resolution—I was wrong, perhaps; God forgive me if I was—but blinded, it may be, and enfeebled in soul by the excess of my anguish, I had made up my mind to abandon this fortress without surrendering it to either party, to claim my children from the rebel princes, and to fly with them into the Corea; but late last night there came a message from the Kumbo-Sama, whose troops I had repulsed, as you know, to warn me that if by a given time I did not place the fortress in his hands, if in the meantime I did not defend it against the rebels, if I yielded one inch of ground to his foes, that he would instantly massacre every Christian in his dominions. The orders are given, the edict prepared, the lives of our brethren hang on a thread. Oh, why has God thus dealt with me? Does not madness lie in this thought? On the one hand my own children, on the other my fathers, my brothers in the faith, the Church my mother, all the hopes of coming years, and the fate of so many thousand souls. Speak, speak, O you on whose lips I have hung with such deep love and reverence, who, with your words of fire, have so often made my heart burn within me, by whose side I have so often longed to die confessing our blessed faith; say, what counsel will you give me; am I to slay my innocent children, or to sign the death-warrant of your brethren and mine?"

The father remained silent for a few moments. If ever an ardent prayer rose up from a human soul to the mercy-seat of God, if ever man pleaded for his fellow-man with that intensity of supplication which is in itself a token that his prayer is heard, he was doing so then. To him there was no perplexity in this question. It stood out before him distinct and clear in the light of duty and in the words of the old French adage, "*Fais ce que dois advienne que pourra.*" But how to put into words the advice he must give, to clear away the mist from that unhappy father's eyes, he hardly knew. God alone could teach him. To Him he was silently, ardently appealing.

Justo could no longer bear the suspense; he fell

at his feet and clung to his knees. "Father," he cried, "might not a man die by his own hand and be forgiven who has such a choice to make?"

"My son, you have no choice to make. God has not left it to you, and still less to me, to decide this question. To what sovereign in this country have you sworn allegiance? To whom have you promised fidelity? For whom, some weeks ago, would you have felt yourself bound to hold this fortress?"

Justo gasped for breath and turned deadly pale, but he looked up steadily in the father's face and said "The Kumbo-Sama."

Father Organtin laid his hand on his head: "My son, that is enough. Do your duty, and leave the consequences to God. Your children are safer in *His* care, even in the King of Arima's court, than if, to shield them from an impending danger, you acted against your conscience."

At that moment a sound of bitter wailing was heard through the fortress, and women's voices, mingled with sobs and loud exclamations, broke upon the silence which had followed the father's last words. Then a heart-rending cry was heard, and the wife and the mother of the chieftan rushed into the apartment striking their breasts and tearing their hair:—"Has the father persuaded thee, O Justo, to give up the fortress to the Emperor, and doom our children to death? Our fair-haired boy, our dark-eyed daughter, the pride and the joy of our house!" exclaimed the unhappy wife.

"Oh, my son!" cried his aged mother, bowing

down before the chieftain and clasping his knees with her trembling hands, "you will kill your parents as well as your children if you do this cruel deed. Father!" she exclaimed, turning wildly towards Father Organtin, "it cannot be that God requires such a sacrifice at his hands!"

"What says my honored father? What says Tacoyama?" asked Justo, taking his mother's hands in his, and raising her from the ground.

Both the weeping women remained silent. At last the younger one said, in a voice broken by sobs, "He is praying before the altar."

"It is there too that we must go," said Justo; and turning to Father Organtin, he made him a sign to lead the way to the chapel.

There the aged Christian Tacoyama was kneeling; his grey head bowed down on his breast. His son knelt down by his side. They had loved each other long and dearly; a more than ordinary mutual affection had united their hearts. From the day when Tacoyama had held his first-born son in his arms and asked for him the blessing of St. Francis Xavier, he had never ceased to form one wish, to put up one prayer, that Justo might be a perfect Christian. Now the day of trial was come. Not the option between life and death, which to one like him would have been but a slight ordeal, but the fiercest of struggles; the most dire of temptations. The old man prayed for his son as Jesus prayed for Peter: that his faith might not fail him.

Hour after hour went by, and the whole of the family and household, men, women, and children, remained on their knees, pleading, with strong crying and tears, to Him who alone could aid them in this their hour of utmost need. Some had recourse to severe penance; others, with the natural fervid eloquence of their race, poured forth aloud heart-rending supplications; even the children did not leave the foot of the altar.

One little boy of five years old, Justo's youngest son, after remaining some time motionless, with his hands clasped and eyes fixed on the Tabernacle, went up gently to his father's side, and whispered softly in his ear—"If the King of Arima cuts off my brother's and my sister's heads, will their souls go to heaven?"

The unhappy father took the child in his arms and clasped him to his breast in silence; but the boy persisted—"If they die, father, will they go to heaven?"

"God forbid we should doubt it," Justo said, in a faltering voice.

"Then it will be very good for them to die, and I wish I was with them. Let me go to the King of Arima, for I should like to kneel down and let him cut off my head; or if he would make for me a little cross, not too big for my size, how pleased I should be; for those who die on a cross, like Jesus, because they love Him so much, are quite sure to go to heaven. O, dear father, let me go!"

A murmur rose at that moment in the lower part

of the chapel, and Justo heard the words, "The father is taking his departure." He wildly started to his feet, and rushed to the entrance hall, where the priest was standing, surrounded by a number of weeping women, who were clinging to his feet and seeking to detain him. Justo hastened to his side; "You must not, you shall not leave us; you are going to a certain death, and your return will be the signal for the publication of the edict and for the massacre of the Christians."

"My son, I pledged my faith to the Emperor that, before noon, I would bring him your answer. If I remain here, my honor is forfeited; my influence for ever at an end with a people whose contempt for a lie nobody can better estimate than you. It is now two hours after midnight; it is high time that I depart. Detain me not, my son; you would commit a grievous crime by involving me in your rebellion against your Sovereign."

"But you sign the death-warrant of our brethren by returning to Meaco without me."

"Oh, Justo!" exclaimed the priest, "would that you could believe, as I do, that God is more powerful than man; that the issues of life and death lie with Him, and not with us, poor miserable creatures that we are! When the patriarch of old led his child up to the heights of Horeb, did he dream in that hour of the angel even then on his way to deliver him from a more appalling trial than even yours this day? Bid these women depart, Justo; as you believe in God, as you are a Christian, do not venture to detain me by force. If you have not the faith or the strength—oh that the God whose servant you have so long been would, even now—"

"Whose servant I *have* been!" cried the unhappy man in a tone of anguish; "have I ceased to be so then? My God! my God! you know I love you!"

Tears were streaming down the pale face of Father Organtin: he was suffering intensely for one who was dearer to him than any of his spiritual children, and he saw that the conflict which Justo was going through was an agonizing one, "Francis! my father, Francis!" he murmured in a low voice, "by thy labors, by thy sufferings, by thy miraculous life, and thy solitary death, plead for this my son. *We* do not deserve to be heard, but we have recourse to *thee*. As thou didst raise the dead through the name of Christ, now, now, by that name of power, strengthen this man's soul."

"Father," Justo said in a tremulous voice, "grant me but one half-hour more; you can spare that time, and yet redeem your pledge. When it has elapsed, you shall depart. Come back with me to the chapel. Besiege for me the throne of grace. Light is beginning to break on the darkness of my spirit."

He bade all leave the chapel save Tacoyama and the priest. No sound was heard in the sacred building. Between his earthly father and his spiritual father Justo Ucondono knelt. Both were pouring forth for him those prayers which have no words, but which rise from the soul like a cry for mercy from a dying man. He too prayed as he had not done since his trial had come upon him. He had asked to be delivered from a great anguish. Now for the first time he surrendered himself into God's hands. "Do with me," he said, "do with them, as seems good to Thee." And when once he had thus prayed, a great calm followed.

There was a solemn and sweet expression in the Christian hero's face as he rose from his knees and left the chapel; his lip did not quiver, there was no shade on his brow, but a steady light in his eye, and a strength not his own in his step; neither mother nor wife ventured to question him; his manner to them was kind and his voice subdued. He sent for the keys of the fortress, and gave them into Tacoyama's hands, "to retain them," he said, "and defend the place against all assailants until such time as our lawful Sovereign the Kumbo-Sama shall send to demand them."

When his intentions were thus made evident, loud cries burst once more from the women and the servants, but Justo was no longer the same man. He gently commanded silence, clasped his wife to his heart, bidding her hope and pray. His little son he took by the hand, and leading him in the midst, he said, "The Scriptures tell us that God has perfected praise out of the mouth of infants. This child's words first awoke me from my dream of despair. Now, father, I am ready to go with you to the Kumbo-Sama.

According to the Eastern fashion, the chieftain prostrated himself on the ground before his aged father. Tacoyama laid his shrivelled hand upon his head. "Justo," he said, "God gives wonderful rewards to faith; we read in the lives of His servants of great miracles wrought for those who did not take their cause in their own hands. He who saved the three young Israelites from the fiery furnace, Daniel from the den of lions, Father Francis from so many perils, may yet rescue your children from the hands of the destroyer."

In silence, but not in gloom; in sadness, but not in despair, the chieftain rode away with Father Organtin from the home where he had gone through such fearful suffering, and where grace had been given to him at last to do God's will and trust the result to Him.

CHAPTER III.

GRACE UCONDONO.

AT the close of a sultry day, amidst groves of orange-trees and oleanders, the Queen and the Princesses of the Court of Arima were enjoying the evening breezes in the gardens of the palace. The quaint peculiarities of Japanese landscape gardening were displayed to the utmost in the grounds of this royal residence. It was a fairy-like scene in which nature and art combined to please the eye and soothe the senses, with images of peaceful repose or graceful animation. Shining alleys, paved with a variety of smooth bright colored stones and bordered by magnificent flowering shrubs and rows of red and white camelias, intersected the grass in every direction. Sparkling cascades fell from artificial rocks, and formed at their feet a number of small lakes, in which gold and silver fishes disported themselves in active idleness. Sculptured representations of animals lurked in the shade of miniature forests, and peeped out of caves and grottoes; whilst cages full of living birds, bearing on their wings the brightest hues of the rainbow, stood in bowers formed by the gnarled and twisted branches of the double blossoming fruit-trees, the victims and the triumphs of Japanese horticulture, devoted to ornament alone, barren of fruit, but prodigal of their pink and white flowers, and taught to thrust at man's bidding their fantastic and lovely boughs into every dwelling, or weave them over every building where he chooses to guide them. On the rising hills which surrounded this "garden of delights" was a wood of dwarf ilex-trees, mingled with rose-bushes and overtopped by a coronal of the three colored planes, that singular production of the Japanese Islands, whose green, red, and yellow foliage stands out in such gorgeous relief against the deep azure of an Eastern sky.

As the ladies of the Court sat reclining on mats in the midst of this fanciful landscape, with their parasols over their heads and their ever-fluttering fans in their hands, they seemed quite in keeping with the scene, almost as artificial in appearance as the carved birds or the sterile blossoms, and as vivacious in their movements as the gilded fish or the buzzing fly. In the midst of them sat their Queen, waited upon with the deference and homage which a royal personage of either sex enjoys as a birth-right in Japan. On her brow there was a settled expression of thought bordering on melancholy. Her deep-set intellectual eyes had a peculiar look, which it was difficult to read, and there was something mournful in the smile which occasionally flitted over her face. Amongst the young girls who surrounded her was one whom she seemed to notice with peculiar distinction, and whose demeanor and countenance was altogether different from that of her other companions. There were two characteristics in her manner which did not belong to any of the other women assembled in that circle ; and though at first sight they may not appear to accord, upon reflection it will be admitted that they usually go together—dignity and humility. The others seemed to move, to act, to feel, at the impulse of the moment ; like playful kittens or chirping birds, timid sheep or shy doves, each, according to her natural character, made a noise or kept silence, reclined lazily on the soft grass with a listless or sleepy eye, indulged in moody melancholy, or chattered in restless excitement, or made the air ring with shouts of laughter, as the fancy seemed to take her —no inward government, no self-imposed restraint intervened between impulses—

> "Variable as the shade
> By the light quiv'ring aspen made,"

and the words or the deeds which resulted from them. There was evidently no established ruler within that unexplored world—their own souls. But on the fair brow of Grace Ucondono—for it was the daughter of the heroic Justo that was seated by the side of the Queen—the qualities so deficient in her companions were visibly impressed. Child-like as was her face, and gay her innocent accents, there was a womanly reserve in her countenance and a subdued sweetness in her voice which could not escape observation, little as those she now associated with could trace it to its source. Although caressed by all the Court, and tenderly loved by the Queen, the Christian maiden and her brother were at that moment captives in the hands of the King of Arima.

At the time when the Governor of Tagacuqui and the six neighboring sovereigns, all vassals like himself of the Emperor, were leagued in close friendship, and the ambitious projects of the latter were not ripe for execution, the sister and brother had been invited to the Court of Arima, in order to witness a tournament of more than ordinary magnificence, at which the feudal chivalry of the neighboring kingdoms was to attend in great numbers, and to display all the splendor of Oriental magnificence. Justo Ucondono accepted the proposal, took part in the martial games, and in an evil hour, at the entreaty of his hosts, left his children behind him, as he thought, for a few days. But under the veil of this warlike entertainment deeper projects were lying. Six of the princes who had met there had formed a conspiracy against the Kumbo-Sama. As Justo Ucondono held at their hands the fortress which was the key of the whole Ximo, they never made a doubt that he would yield it up to them, and their fury was in proportion great when they found that not only he refused to join in their conspiracy, but to surrender what they chose to consider their own property, though, in fact, they themselves only held it as vassals of the Emperor.

The fierce Marindono, King of Firando, the soul of the whole rebellion, vowed that the possession of that stronghold and the co-operation of Justo was necessary to its success, and he made the King of Arima bind himself to his colleagues not to yield up the children of his friend until their demands were complied with. They were to answer with their innocent lives for their father's adherence to the cause of the conspirators. With some natural virtues, capable of good impulses, and even of generous sacrifices, these heathen warriors and statesmen possessed none of the principles of rectitude which grow out of the Christian religion, and are traceable to its influence even when acted upon by men who barely recognize its sway, but yet are unconsciously ruled by the teachings of the Church. Fondasadono did not hesitate to comply with the exigencies of his allies, and Grace and Francis Ucondono remained as hostages at that Court where they had been invited as guests.

They were partly unconscious of their position, and, though longing to return to their home, and wondering day after day that their father did not send for them, and troubled with fear and misgivings as to his silence, they little dreamed of the dangers that were threatening them, or of his suffering on their account. To these young Christians their prolonged residence amongst idolaters was a severe trial. They could not speak freely of their faith. They witnessed acts and heard language which filled them with burning indignation. The

eyes of the boy flashed, and his sister's filled with
tears, when the poor were spoken of with contempt,
and the weak treated with cruelty. Religion had
opened their eyes, young as they were, to the
enormities practised or tolerated by their countrymen. It was with a wonderful eloquence that the
Christian maiden spoke of the sanctity of marriage,
when her companions used language in keeping
with the infallible degradation of woman in a
country where plurality of wives and the practice
of divorce is permitted. With a flushing cheek and
a throbbing heart she heard them speak of children
doomed to death by their parents for some natural
defect, from avarice, or caprice, and left to perish
by the cold river side or in the gloomy depths of
the forest.

"Have you heard," said one of the Princesses of
Fondasadono's family on the evening when they
were sitting in the bower of roses on the terrace of
the palace—"have you heard, ladies, that Grace
Ucondono sometimes leaves her father's abode at
break of day, when the dew is still hanging on the
leaves, and the early breeze stirring the branches
of the three colored planes? Guess what treasures
she goes in search of. You think, perhaps, that it
is the stone which glitters more brightly in the
sunshine than the dewdrop on the rose, or the fiery
blossoms of the champaka, which only bloom at the
early dawn, or the delicate fern which waves to and
fro on the edge of the rock, or the butterfly that
glitters like a living jewel in the fresh morning

air? No, ladies, the treasures she seeks are dying
infants; creatures discarded by their own parents,
surely the only beings who can care to see them
live. And what do you think she does with them?
She sends them to the foreign bonzes and the
black-robed women they direct, who rear these
wretched babes in their own superstition. I have
been even told that she has been known to wash
them with her own hands, for some purpose she
could best tell us, when they had been all but dead,
and there was no time to take them to a bonze."
There was much laughter among the hearers of this
speech. The Queen, however, did not join in it—
a burning spot appeared on her sallow cheek, and
deepened and deepened in hue till it seemed to glow
like fire.

Grace smiled one of those smiles which have in
them the deepest sadness this earth can know, and
the highest joy which heaven can give — the
"Miserere" for those who lie in darkness and
cannot see; the "Deo gratias" for the faith which
daily saves so many souls.

She spoke out that day; and from her young lips
truths flowed to which the sages of Greece and the
orators of Rome might have listened with wonder
and with awe. She was the daughter of a line of
heroes. Her grandfather had been one of the first
Christians of Japan, and the friend of St. Francis.
She had been nurtured in the faith of Christ; and
as she stood there in that luxurious garden, in the
midst of the dark-eyed, and many of them high-

souled women of her own land, preaching the gospel from the very depths of her heart, a brighter picture of human loveliness and celestial beauty could hardly be conceived.

That very day before the Queen had left the garden, and even whilst Grace was still speaking, a murmur was heard in the courts adjacent to the palace, and Francis Ucondono, a mere boy in age and in appearance, entered the royal gardens, and after making obeisance to the Queen, turned to his sister, and said in a joyous voice, "Good news, dear Grace! good news! our grandfather has just arrived, and, wonderful to relate, Father Organtin with him! But they will not let me see them yet. I should not have known they were here, but from the eastern turret where I was mending my bow and arrows I saw them riding through the archway. My joy was so great that I would fain have leapt out of window and fallen at their feet; my good angel restrained me, however, and when I was told they had gone to the King, and that I must refrain my impatience, I bethought me of running to you with the good news, and so rudely broke into her Majesty's presence," the boy added, with an ingenuous blush and smile, and another profound bow to the Queen.

"They are doubtless come with some important news from Tagacuqui," said one of the Princesses.

"But I wonder," said the Queen, with a look of uneasiness, "that it is Tacoyama and not his son who has come to confer with the assembled kings.

He has of late abandoned all matters of state to Justo Ucondono's jurisdiction and this Christian bonze. What brings him here? Did you not say, Francis, that one of the foreign priests is with your grandfather? The kings have been impatiently waiting for a messenger from Tagacuqui."

"Melia," she said in a low voice to one of her ladies, "go into the palace, and ask the governor of the household if aught has transpired as to the purport of this conference."

The lady in waiting retired, and when some of the young Princesses began to converse, the Queen peremptorily enjoined silence, as if too much agitated to endure the sound of their voices; she fluttered her fan with a vehemence which betrayed nervous anxiety. The Christian boy and girl spoke to each other in a whisper, and were about to move to a little distance from the bower, but the Queen called to them to return and sit at her feet. Her agitation became so great that she could no longer conceal it, and they began to perceive that some important event was at hand.

The lady who had been sent to the palace now returned, with one of the officers of the Court, who informed her Majesty that the King desired that the children of Justo Ucondono should be conducted to the Hall, where, conjointly with the allied Princes, he was giving audience to the Governor of Tagacuqui and the foreign bonze.

The Queen turned very pale, and embraced Grace with the greatest tenderness. "Your words just now," she whispered, "cut me to the heart. I had a child who was born blind. They took it away from me, and doomed it to death. It was the anguish of that remembrance that made me writhe when they were speaking of those low-born infants you seek to rescue from the grave; mine was a royal and a beautiful babe, but they would not suffer it to live. The first-born of a king, they said, must be free from every blemish. He is gone from me, my loved one, and the gods have denied me children, though I performed two years ago the great pilgrimage to Ozin, and sat in the seat of fate, suspended over the dread abyss. Oh, Grace, dearest Grace, would I were a Christian!"

A wildness came over the unhappy mother's face as she rapidly uttered these words. She kept hold of Grace's hand, as if she would fain have detained her who had been the means of rescuing so many children from an untimely death. But the officer in waiting reminded her of the King's orders, and the brother and sister were hurried away to the Hall of State.

It was with a shudder that the aged chieftain saw those beloved ones, his son's beautiful children, advancing towards him with joyous faces and with outstretched arms. They prostrated themselves at his and Father Organtin's feet. The latter blessed them fervently, and bade them stand by their grandfather's side and listen to his words with calm and strong hearts. "Now," he said to his aged friend, "now is the time to speak, my friend. I will engage for these children that they will rejoice to hear of their father's noble conduct, even though it may be the means of placing their own lives in jeopardy." He fixed his eyes, as he said these words, on Grace and Francis, and the bright eager glance which answered his gave instant confirmation to his words.

Tacoyama raised his eyes to heaven. "My son," he began in a voice which faltered with age and with emotion ; and then he paused as if unable to proceed. The silence which ensued was ominous. The faces of the rebel princes were turned upon him with a fierce and intense anxiety, and Morondono's eyes glared like those of a lion about to be robbed of his prey. "My son," he repeated in a firmer voice, "has left Tagacuqui, and is on his way to Meaco. The fortress will be to-night in the hands of the Kumbo-Sama."

For an instant no one spoke. It was like the stillness which precedes the storm. Then a deep, hoarse murmur rose amongst that crowd of conspirators, which was gradually taken up by their retainers, until it grew into a yell wild as a warcry, stern as a sentence of death.

"The curses of the gods light upon him and his race!" cried a hundred voices at once. "Let his children perish, and his name be blotted out of the land."

The King of Arima advanced towards the old chieftain and addressed him in a tone of passionate adjuration. "Depart, old man; depart from these halls, where you have come as an envoy, and may not therefore be struck down by the vengeful swords of Arima; go hence in safety: but when from every watch-tower and every height we have lost sight of your retreating forms, then armed men on swift steeds shall scour the plain, and, like the lightning, overtake you ere you reach the threshold of that palace, the scene of your son's treachery."

The little hand that Father Organtin held quivered in his grasp, and a crimson flush o'erspread the face of Justo Ucondono's son.

Then the fierce Morondono spoke: "These children must die; six kings in arms are not to be defied in vain, not betrayed with impunity."

Tacoyama leant on his stick and tried to speak, but his strength failed him. Young Francis whispered to Father Organtin, "Before they put us to death, father, tell these kings, in our presence, that our father is no traitor."

The priest released the boy's hand and advanced towards the princes, whose eyes were still flashing with rage, or gloomily bent on the ground, and thus addressed them in their own language: "Revenge is sweet to the natural heart of man. It is a wild sort of justice which those have recourse to who do not adore a god to whom they can trust their own cause. Kings and Princes, I am not come here to argue, or to dispute, but to offer myself to you as the just object of that revenge which you are seeking to satisfy. I am not Justo

Ucondono's envoy; I never came here in that
character. I am simply your prisoner. These
children have never offended you; they have been
like innocent lambs in your hands. Why should
they perish? Here is the man who has dared to
challenge your indignation; here is the man who
persuaded the noble Justo to act as he has done;
who reminded him that life is short and eternity
long; who induced him to expose the lives of his
children rather than act against his conscience.
Accept my life, noble Princes; shed the blood of a
stranger who despises your idols and believes in
one only God, and spare the old man who has lived
amongst you for nearly fourscore years, and borne
an honored name in the records of your country.
Spare the son of Justo Ucondono, who has fought
side by side with you in many a hard-won field,
and who, when he abandoned your cause, did so at
the price of such anguish that his black hair in a
few hours was tinged with white. Spare the
maiden who has dwelt in your halls and shared
your children's sports—spare the aged, spare the
feeble, spare the young!"

Father Organtin's voice had been clear, loud and
strong until he uttered these last words; then it
began to falter, and he stopped. His eyes were
fixed on the man he was addressing with that peculiar expression which belongs to those who have
led austere lives, and by strict self-discipline have
subdued in themselves every unruly passion and
inordinate impulse. The man who lives for God

alone unconsciously governs others while he only aims at ruling himself. In the case of some great saints, that influence has extended to the brute creation. The wild beasts of the forests and the birds of the air were as submissive to St. Francis of Assissi as to Adam in the garden of Eden; and the successor of the Apostle of the Indies, the calm, gentle missionary priest, whose powerful and highly cultivated intellect and ardent soul had long been schooled into entire subserviency to the sole end of man's creation—God's glory and His service—stood that day before that group of angry men with all the security of one who knew that the worst that could happen to him was to die; a very small thing indeed to those who have made the conquest of self the business of a whole lifetime.

His words had been few, but they had fallen on the ears of men who had a keen appreciation of heroism.

There was a natural magnanimity about the Japanese character which made them susceptible of admiration for an act of self-devotion, and the passions which had so fiercely raged a moment before were now subsiding like the waves when the tide is beginning to turn.

Tacoyama and his son were beloved and respected by their neighbors, and the children of Justo had excited a strong interest in the breast of Fondasadono and his family, which was acting favorably at this moment. The generosity of the Christian bonze, as they called him, so unlike what they had ever seen in the native priests, who abjured the world and its ties in order to win the respect of the vulgar, whilst they all but openly indulged in the grossest immoralities, made a singular impression upon them. He looked so like a being of a higher order, whilst he pleaded for those he loved and called his children.

Some of these princes knew something of the Christian faith; they remembered the wonderful story of a God dying for His creatures, and as they looked upon Father Organtin that day, something whispered to their hearts that he was indeed the servant of that God. O man, where is thy strength, where is the force of thy purposes, when God sends one of His angels to lay his hand on thy uplifted arm, and by a whisper from on high to soften thy blind wrath?

A voice very like an angel's rose on the silence which had followed the father's words. Grace left the place where she had been standing all the time by Tacoyama's side, and knelt down at the feet of the priest. "Father," she said, "what words have you been speaking? What right have you to give away a life which belongs to all the Christians of Japan, for mine and my little brother's?" We are helpless children, who can do no good to any one; and if our parents weep for us for a few days, they will soon be comforted. If we do not return to them, they will come to us. But, father, if you die, who will there be to speak to our poor countrymen the words of salvation as you have done?

They will kneel down by your grave, and listen in vain for your voice. Never again will it say to the sinner, 'My child, God forgives thee ;' 'My child, go in peace, and sin no more ;' or speak of the sacred heart of Jesus, and the love of Mary, till tears fall from their eyes and their hearts are on fire. No, father, you must not die; you must live to save many souls ; and if Francis and I are put to death, because our dear father obeyed God rather than men, we will kiss your feet, receive your blessing, and then kneel down side by side, and joyfully wait for the stroke which will sever our heads from our bodies, and send our souls to heaven."

Francis hastened to his sister's side, put his arm round her neck, and both knelt down and repeated in a low voice the "Our Father."

Loud cries were heard at that moment from the inside of the palace. The wife and the sisters of the King of Arima had been cut to the heart by the report which had spread through the women's apartments, that their young guests were sentenced to death, and were rending the air with their lamentations.

Almost at the same time a messenger reached the fortress, who brought tidings of the approach of the Kumbo-Sama with a powerful force. Some of the allied princes, who had remained unmoved by the generosity of the Christian captives and the innocence of the children, became alive to the fear that in case of defeat they would shut out all possibility of making favorable terms if they proceeded to extremities with their prisoners; they consented, therefore, to the proposal of the King of Arima, that they should be, for the present, removed with their grandfather and the Christian priest to one of the apartments of the palace.

On the following night the Queen, with the consent of her husband, as was generally supposed, procured for them the means of escape. They fled across the plains between Arima and Meaco. As the Japanese children gazed on the blue vault of heaven, with its myriads of stars, and the glorious moon shedding its silvery light on the valleys of the Ximo, their souls seemed to yearn for those blissful regions which had seemed so near at hand.

"Grace," said Father Organtin to the maiden, whose thoughts he read, "a few hours ago you were standing on the heights of Thabor, and heaven seemed within your reach; but it has to be won, my child, by a longer and drearier road—you may have to go through Calvary ere you draw so near to it again."

When Justo Ucondono received his children back from the jaws of death, as it seemed to him, he exclaimed, "Oh, father, you were right; God's ways are not as our ways, nor His thoughts like our thoughts. It is very good to trust Him. The Emperor has indeed been kind to me; but I was like Rachel, and refused to be comforted, because of my children; sorrow endured for a night, but joy has come in the morning."

"But to go straight to heaven would be the greatest joy of all, dear father," said his son. The chieftain laid his hand on his head in silence. The child's words were unanswerable.

CHAPTER IV.

A VISIT TO THE PALACE.

LAURENTIA had accomplished her visit to the palace. The success of her brother's fans had been complete. She had displayed the whole contents of the casket before the Empress and the ladies of the Court. The beauty of the paintings had been extolled, and the good taste with which the tassels were adapted to each, according to their shape and color, noticed and admired. When those which bore the emblems of the Christian faith were produced, some curiosity was excited. The Empress looked at them long and earnestly, but made no remark. When Laurentia timidly pointed out the one which had been copied from King Bartholomew's favorite picture, she said with a sigh, "The King of Omura is a wise and valiant prince," and then hastily adverted to another subject. Laurentia, nothing daunted, spoke of the impression which that picture had made on the heart of that monarch, and of the share it had in his conversion. But one of the elderly ladies of the Court dryly observed, "That the Kumbo-Sama tolerated, indeed, the foreign religion in such of his subjects as were faithful and useful servants of the Crown; but that as a topic of conversation it was not acceptable at Court."

The Empress looked annoyed at this remark, and said to one of her attendants, "In return for the pleasure which the inspection of these ingenious works of art have afforded us, we will feast this maiden's eyes with the sight of the presents which the youthful Ambassador Mancia Ito has brought to us from Europe; one who has so much taste as she displays in setting off these lovely fans to the best advantage cannot but be delighted with the beautiful things which our envoy has lately laid at our feet with loving messages from the European Sovereigns, and the blessings of the great high priest of the Christian faith."

Two of the ladies in waiting complied with the orders of the Empress, and having brought a large chest into the room, they proceeded to spread out on a gold fringed carpet the treasures to which she had alluded.

When the Japanese embassy had been mentioned, Laurentia's cheeks had flushed, and as she stooped, to hide her face, the beating of her heart was almost audible. She vainly tried to wrap in silver-paper the fans that were lying near her; her hands trembled too much.

It was now more than two years since the day that she had stood in the port of Nangazaqui watching with straining eyes the ship on board of which Mancia Ito, his colleagues, and his suite, had set sail for Goa on their way to Europe. Amongst the pages of the young Ambassador was Isafai, the son of their next dear neighbor, and the playmate of her childhood. They had loved each other since the time that from each side of the trellised barrier which divided the two little gardens of their respective homes they had pelted each other with the fallen blossoms of the peach and almond trees, shared their sweetmeats, or played at ball with oranges and pomegranates.

When they grew up, Isafai would fain have wedded the companion of his childish sports, but Laurentia turned a deaf ear to his suit; not that she had ceased to love him—the daughter of the Capulets was not more tenderly attached to the heir of the Montagues than this Japanese maiden to the highly gifted and spirited Isafai. The glance of his dark eyes, the smile that beamed on his expressive countenance, were as beautiful to her as the summer lightning in the western sky, or the first rays of sunshine on a lovely morning in spring. She would willingly have surrendered for his sake every enjoyment this world could afford; but her heavenly hopes, her faith, her divine privileges, she never dreamt could be foregone; she could not have wounded the Sacred Heart which had been wounded for her for the sake of any human affection, however ardent, however pure.

It was not a sacrifice she made, for it had never occurred to her as a possibility that a Christian could marry a heathen, a child of the Church one of its enemies.

Vainly did Isafai plead long and earnestly; in vain did he promise her the free exercise of her religion, and that he would never bring to his home any other wife but herself, and never on any account divorce or forsake her; in vain he wept at her feet and implored her to relent. She looked upon him with a pitying tenderness which gave an almost heavenly sweetness to her countenance, but it was the look which the angel at the gate of Paradise might have turned upon the children of men pleading for entrance to the Eden they had forfeited. She did not, she could not, have yielded. Nor would he seek the only means through which he might have obtained the blessing he so earnestly desired. He would not examine into the truth of the Christian religion. He refused to study its laws, or to confer with its teachers. In common with many of his countrymen, a proud sense of honor was the ruling passion of Isafai; and though he did not rank with the nobles of Japan, he shared in the spirit which prevailed amongst them, and spurned to make a concession which he considered degrading. He preferred any amount of suffering to aught that savored of humiliation. In abandoning Laurentia he was offering up a greater sacrifice to his pride than is often made by men to conscience and to God. It is not always true that men sin because they will not submit to suffering; they often suffer, keenly, cruelly, under the sway of the father of lies. Since the day that he fell himself, like lightning from heaven, it is his policy to blind men in order to ruin them.

Proudly and silently Isafai took leave of the Christain maiden whom he had loved long and well; whom he had loved for those very virtues, that sweet modesty, that tender womanly charity, that nobility of soul, which were due to the very faith he so intensely hated. Nor was he altogether ignorant of the cause of her superiority to the heathen daughters of the land. He would not, strange to say, have had her renounce the Christian faith. Like so many inconsistent men, he would have wished her to retain her belief in Christ and act in opposition to His laws. He had an instinctive feeling that had she bent the knee to the divinities of Japan, and joined in the worship of Arima and Cosca,—that had she been under the influence of the low-minded, though often learned and eloquent, ministers of that foul superstition, she would have lost in his eyes, if not the beauty which attracted, at least the charm which subdued his heart. Often and often he had watched her on her way back from the Christian church, and wondered, to borrow words from the American poet,

"That a celestial brightness, a more etherial beauty,
Shone on her face and encircled her form when, after confession, Homeward serenely she walked with God's benediction upon her."

"When she had passed," it seemed indeed to him, "like the ceasing of exquisite music."

He had seen her go into the abodes of sickness and poverty with a strange mixture of feelings, half disgusted, half admiring; the prejudices of his country and education striving with that intuitive sense of virtue which exists in the natural man when the practice of vice has not blunted its perceptions. "Strange! unnatural!" he would exclaim, as he saw her bending over some poor wretch covered with a loathsome disease, or gently closing the eyes of some dying sufferer. And yet he would not have interfered to withdraw her from those singular pursuits. He thought she never looked so beautiful as at those moments. But he would not be touched; he would not admit the first ray of light into his soul which by degrees would have enlightened it. He forcibly shut out the truth, "refusing to hear the voice of the charmer, charm he never so wisely." At last the mental conflict grew too hard to endure, and he broke away from an influence which irritated his pride and wounded his feelings.

The Japanese Embassy was at that time about to sail for Europe. He offered himself to accompany Mancia Ito, one of the envoys, as his page, and the offer was accepted. The ship set sail from Nangazaqui, bearing away one proud and aching heart to those unknown regions which seemed to the Japanese almost as untangible as the world beyond the grave; whilst another was left behind, steeped in so much sorrow and suffering that it required all the elasticity of youth and of a naturally buoyant disposition to overcome in some measure the effects of that grief; but nursing at the same time a cherished hope, laid before God every day in prayer, and for the attainment of which, life, and more than life, was continually offered up.

The report of the return of the Embassy had reached Meaco. The envoys had met the Emperor at Ozaca, and there laid at his feet the gifts which the European monarchs had sent to the Sovereign of Japan. None of the Ambassador's suite had yet arrived at the capital. Laurentia had only heard that Mancia Ito had entered the novitiate of the Jesuits, and was residing at their house at Ozaca. Of his page she could learn no tidings. The sight of the curious and beautiful articles of European manufacture now spread out before her seemed a reminiscence of him whom she had accompanied in thought to those distant climes which had been to her like a land of dreams and shadowy visions. One by one she examined them with an admiring curiosity. There was the casket enriched with jewels and surmounted with the initials of the Catholic King; the vase from the royal manufactory at Sevres, the present of his most Christian Majesty; the inlaid marble table from Florence; the rare and quaintly-mounted gems from Venice; the copies of famous pictures from the galleries of Rome and Bologna; but what, above all, riveted her eyes and engaged her attention was the Missal which the Holy Father had destined for the late Emperor, who, when the Embassy had sailed from Japan, was on the verge of becoming a Christian.

The triple crown and the keys were stamped in gold on the binding, and each page was illustrated by magnificently painted designs. The Empress desired this rare volume to be opened, and told Laurentia to explain the meaning of the pictures. Now the opportunity for which the young catechist had watched and prayed was at last afforded. The elderly lady in waiting had withdrawn when the European treasures were produced. She hated the very name of foreign lands, and had never ceased to lament the intercourse recently established with the kingdoms of the Continent. The other ladies gathered round Laurentia, who related with touching simplicity the history of the birth, of the miracles, and of the Passion of Christ. It seemed to her incredibly strange to be speaking, within the very palace walls, of those glorious truths, and to be holding in her hands the very book which the Vicar of Christ had with his own hands given into Mancia Ito's care, for the Empress had told her this, and repeated the Holy Father's words; how he had blessed the young envoy, and told him to assure his countrymen of the love he felt for them, his new children; how he prayed for them every day at the tomb of the apostles.

"The bearer of that message," said Laurentia, "has devoted himself, if report speaks truly, to the delivery of Christ's message to men. He has laid aside the robes of state, and all the courtly splendor which has so long surrounded him, to put on the black robe of our fathers, and sit at their feet in humble subjection."

"It is as you say," answered the Empress; "and passing strange is such an act in a man in the flower of his age and on the high road to fortune."

"This book," said Laurentia, laying her hand on the Missal, "this book speaks of a broad road that leads to destruction, and a narrow one that leads to life. Perhaps Mancia Ito preferred the latter."

"Child," exclaimed the Empress, half provoked and half amused, "it hardly becomes your youth and sex to discourse so like an aged bonze."

Laurentia colored, and said, with a sweet smile, "It is also written in this book, that God chooses the weak and the foolish ones in this world to confound the wise and the strong."

The Empress sighed, and ordered her attendants to remove the regal presents; and whilst they were doing so, she beckoned to Laurentia to come nearer to her. "Maiden," she said, "I have been ere now almost persuaded to be a Christian, and all that relates to your strange faith is like music to me, sweet in my ears and soothing to my soul; but I am not a free agent. The Kumbo-Sama would kill me if I embraced a religion he proscribes."

"But believes in himself," said Laurentia boldly.

"No," replied the Empresss, "he does not. Our bonzes he despises; but he mistrusts all priests, and now there are grand schemes in his mind which your religion stands in the way of, and in consequence he is beginning to hate it, though he is personally much attached to your fathers, especially to his interpreter, Father Rodriguez. But hearken now, Laurentia, to what I am about to say. I should like to have a Christian near me who would sometimes speak to me in secret of Him whom you call the only true God, and who, if I was in danger of death, would open to me the gates of heaven by the means you spoke of a moment ago. I will attach both you and your brother to my service. In a few days the Emperor, attended by all the Court, proceeds to Fuximi, there to inspect the preparations he is making for the reception of the Chinese Ambassadors. Nothing that the eye of man has ever yet witnessed approaches to the magnificence which he is about to display on this occasion. Thousands of palaces are rising at his bidding on the plains between Meaco and Ozaca. Theatres of a size which baffle all conception. Temples more gorgeous by far than those which Nobunanga destroyed on the hills of Frenoxama; and on an altar raised above all others, amidst the time-honored images of the divinities of Japan, one larger and more stately than the rest, that of the reigning sovereign, is to be set up and worshipped by his people."

Laurentia turned pale, and the Empress perceived it. "Child, what ails you?" she kindly said. As the maiden did not immediately answer, she added, "We wish you to accompany us in this journey. We choose your brother also to attend us. Go

home now and announce to him that he is to follow
in our train, and take sketches of the gorgeous
scenes which will unfold themselves before his eyes
during this royal progress. The governor of our
household will furnish you both with the necessary
equipments for your new position. I shall commit
to you, maiden, the custody of the imperial fans as
your ostensible office in my household."

Laurentia knelt at the feet of the Empress, and
touched the ground with her forehead.

As she passed on her way home through the
noisy streets it felt as if her brain could hardly
master the multitude of thoughts which were
crowding into it. Ozaca, was she indeed to travel
thither, where, in spite of herself, her mind was
ever dwelling? Then the Empress! what a task
was before her: to win, by word, by example, by
daily silent prayer, that soul which was struggling
for freedom, but held in the iron bondage of terror
and human respect. Her brother, too! to be about
the Court, and have full scope for the exercise of
his really remarkable talents: this had been long
the object of his ambition ; with what joy he would
receive the announcement! Then there came a
thought which froze the blood in her veins—that
daring act of idolatry ! That open outrage about
to be offered to the Majesty of the Eternal God!
It seemed to cast a dark shade on her spirit; it
oppressed her with a strange, dull, heavy weight.
She could hardly account to herself for the way in
which it haunted her, for she lived, alas ! amongst

heathens, and daily witnessed their idolatries without the sickening feeling that came over her then.

She had no sooner reached home, and had hardly had time to make known to Matthias the news of his appointment and her own, which was received by him with the most rapturous delight, than an officer from the Court arrived and confirmed the news. The brother and sister conversed long and earnestly that evening. It was a great change that had come over their lives. Both indulged in a variety of anticipations connected with it; he rejoiced in his sister's courage in going to the palace; he owned that her boldness had been far more successful in every sense than his prudence would have been; he congratulated her on the good she might do in her new position, and expressed an earnest hope that he might also serve the interests of religion by the exercise of his art and the assistance he might afford to other Christians when once his talents had secured him influence at Court. He was full of good resolutions and fervent thoughts that night. If things went well with him he was willing to pay tribute, as it were, in the shape of pious feelings and virtuous intentions.

His sister was less excited, more thoughtful; she made fewer plans for the future; and when she was once more alone that night, if any one could have seen her face, they would have wondered if it was joy or fear, or hope or grief that was causing such swift shadows to pass over her brow like the clouds over the moon on a stormy night.

The day before her departure from Meaco and her entrance on her new position in the Japanese household, she had the happiness of once more beholding Grace Ucondono, who had returned with her grandfather to his palace in that city. These two Christian maidens, of very different rank, but united by the bond of their common faith, had maintained a strict friendship since the days of childhood, when they had both attended the catechism class in the father's chapel. Both had also long been devoted to the work of rescuing abandoned children from an untimely death, or, if that was impossible, of opening heaven to them through the sacrament of Baptism. Under the guidance of a pious matron, the wife of Andre the archer, they had formed an association for this purpose. At the feet of Father Organtin they had offered themselves, in God's presence and in the sight of His holy Mother and all the men and women saints in the heavenly court, to imitate Christ in bearing injuries, in leading a life of poverty, spiritual or actual, and especially to labor for poor children. This promise they regarded as a solemn dedication to a most holy work. They felt that it was recorded on high. Often their minds were haunted by the thought of the perishing infant; the unbaptized babe, the lonely riverside, the dark dismal marsh where human life and human souls were in jeopardy.

Alas! the same cries ring in our ears even now! the same dismal echoes rise, not from the solitary muir, or the wild sea-beach, but from the foul alleys and dark recesses of a densely-peopled city. We, too, have to mourn not so much for children left to die by unnatural parents, for, alas! such is the misery and the crime that surges around the homes of our poor, that death in infancy we must often look upon as one of God's highest mercies—but over those doomed to vice and unbelief by fatal neglect.

This little band of Christian women were wont to meet at the house of Agatha, the wife of Andre Ongasamara, a man of high birth but decayed fortunes, who supported himself by teaching young men to ride, and to shoot with bow and arrow. In no country was nobility of descent more in esteem than in Japan; but the loss of fortune in no way diminished the respect with which a man was treated whose rank in the state had been at any time acknowledged. Andre was greatly looked up to, not only by the Christians, but by his countrymen in general. His father, who had been a renowned warrior in his day, and was now in his eightieth year, had been recently received into the Church. His wife, the good Agatha, had long been regarded by the Christian women of Meaco with the sort of love and veneration which St. Frances of Rome inspired in her day, or the pious Madame Acarie at that very time in Paris. She was the leader in all charitable undertakings; the advocate of the poor, and the consoler of the afflicted, she oftened travelled great distances, suffering the while incredible hardships, in order to visit some of those small communities of Christians who seldom could enjoy the ministrations of a priest, but who patiently kept the faith and supplied by religious exercises, humbly and faithfully performed for the scanty amount of sacramental advantages afforded them. She gave them every consolation that sympathy and encouragement could offer under such circumstances, and thus remained in active communication with numbers of Christians scattered over the land.

Her great allies and firmest friends were Matthew the blind comb-seller, and another old man, an itinerant musician, who, by charming the ears of the peasantry, in whom the love of music was a perfect passion, often found a way to their hearts, and won them to the faith by his touching expostulations and sweet words about God.

Meeting as usual in Agatha's humble abode, the little band of Christian women rejoiced that day at the return of the long absent daughter of Justo Ucondono. She did not speak of the dangers she had been exposed to, but only asked that some prayers might be said in thanksgiving for a great mercy received. Laurentia's appointment in the Empress' household was then discussed, and advice given to her as to the line of conduct to pursue in that difficult position. Combining, Agatha said, with a smile, "the wisdom of the serpent with the simplicity of the dove."

"Mother," said Grace to her friend, for she always gave her that name, "can you call to mind the circumstances which Anselm, the flute-player, related to us, about five or six years ago, about a child whom he rescued from a watery grave in the kingdom of Arima?"

"That is indeed taxing my memory severely, dear Grace. We have, thank God, rescued so many infants since that time, that I can scarcely remember the circumstances of each particular case."

"It was almost the first time I ever came to your house that Anselm, who happened to be present, related this story, and so I suppose it has remained fixed on my recollection. He said, I think, that one morning, at break of day, he was walking by the side of the river which flows through the town of Arima, and that much lower down, and nearer to the sea, he saw something floating on the water which resembled one of the little osier boats in which infants are so often left to die. It was far beyond his reach; he could not swim, and no boat was at hand. In the very centre of the wide stream, borne onward by the current and the breeze, that tiny craft was making its straight and fatal way to the ocean, freighted, it might be, with the dying body and the unbaptized soul of a child. He told us, in his simple way, that he knelt down on the shore, and invoked Father Francis, praying him by the great love he had for souls whilst he was on earth, to obtain, that if a child was indeed thus drifting to destruction it might yet be rescued and baptized. No sooner had he uttered the words than a gust of wind changed the direction of the floating cradle, and soon it lay entangled in the rushes of the shore. He found a beautiful infant lying in this sad cot dressed in costly robes."

"I now remember those facts, dear Grace," said Agatha, "exactly as you relate them. They had quite escaped my memory; but what makes you revert to them now?"

"I have a reason, dear mother, for greatly wishing to discover what became of that infant, and whether the clothes which it wore have been preserved. Do you soon expect to see Anselm?"

"He has not been in Meaco for several months; when last I heard of him he was in the kingdom of Bungo. He generally visits us towards the time of the Feast of our Lady's Nativity. Laurentia may perhaps see him at Ozaca, it is his habit to frequent places where people assemble together on public occasions. His vocation is to be in a crowd. The desert and the forest have no attractions for him; he must be where he can work for men, and come in contact with them: his love of souls is restless. When he heard one of the fathers relate that their great founder said that if God gave him his choice, to die at once and go to heaven, or to stay on earth, still uncertain as to his salvation, but gaining more souls to Christ, he should not hesitate to remain, Anselm's eyes beamed with joy, and he said with great simplicity—'I would do like St. Ignatius.'—My children," she continued, "have you heard that the Kumbo-Sama has resolved to put up a statue of himself in the gigantic temple which he is erecting near Ozaca, and that he intends to call upon all his subjects to pay it religious worship? His predecessors have been contented to be adored *after* death, but he intends to enjoy that privilege during his lifetime. He is determined that the Chinese Ambassadors shall witness that homage paid to him. They speak of an edict compelling all persons, under pain of death, to comply with this obligation."

Grace and Laurentia smiled. "Then he will have to put to death many thousands of his subjects," said the former.

"The rivers of Japan will flow with blood," exclaimed the latter.

"The gates of heaven will open wide to receive a noble band of martyrs," cried another.

"Ladies," said a plain, quiet little woman, who seldom opened her lips, but was a great deal in the church, and instructed poor converts, "I have a favor to ask you. Will you promise to grant it?"

"I think we may safely do so, good Catherine," said Agatha with a smile. "But tell us—what is it?"

"If, when the edict is published and the crosses

are erected, you should see me turn pale and look frightened, will you please gag my mouth and drag me to the place of execution? And, whatever I may say or do at the time, be sure you do not let me go."

Having delivered herself of this speech, the little woman sank back into her previous silence, and though her friends laughed, they felt there was both wisdom and holiness in the poor little catechist's words.

Meanwhile another assembly was being held at the palace of Guenifoin, the Governor of the city. Justo Ucondono, Simon Condera, Austin the High Admiral, and many other persons of rank, both Christian and heathen, had met together to consult upon the preparations they had made, and were still making, in obedience to the Kumbo-Sama's orders, in order to second, by an extraordinary display of splendor, his wishes with regard to the reception of the Chinese Ambassadors. It especially behoved the Christian noblemen not to be behindhand on these occasions, as they would easily have been accused of indifference to the national glory; for, even when best pleased with their services, the Sovereigns always looked upon them with a jealous and suspicious eye. They felt that there was a point beyond which they could not command their submission; that they owed an allegiance to a Heavenly Master. The Emperor had been sharp-sighted enough to discern that if in the recent struggle with the rebel princes, whom, when once in possession of the stronghold of Tagacuqui, he had easily reduced to obedience, Justo's conscience had been enlisted on the opposite side, he might as vainly have attempted to repulse the advancing tide, or to remove the mountains of Saxuma into the sea, as have compelled him to submit.

The Christian lords foresaw that a conflict would arise between them and the Imperial despot on the day when in the madness of his pride the Kumbo-Sama would call upon them to pay religious worship to his statue. Not one of these earnest and high-spirited men shrank from the trial; but they were determined not to give him an excuse for taxing them with indifference to the interest of their country; aud though many of them were straitened in fortune from the losses they had endured during the last persecutions, and the sacrifices they had made in order to rebuild their ruined churches; though they were careless of display in worldly matters, and full of other thoughts and anxieties than the exhibition of military pomp, the vain festivities, the empty pageantry of theatrical representations which was to dazzle the eyes of strangers and conceal the rankling evils of inward discord and heathen demoralization, they took part in these deliberations and sacrificed their own tastes to what, under the circumstances, appeared to them a duty.

Guenifoin, the Governor or Viceroy of Meaco, was most anxious that the Christians should appear to advantage on this occasion. He was not one himself, although he loved them well. He was one of those men who have a heart to feel the beauty of goodness, and a mind capable of discerning the truth, but the world was uppermost in his sympathies and affections; it clung to him like Dejanira's robe. To tear off that magic garment in which he had been clothed from his youth up, would have been a torture he dared not face; the shame of the Cross was more than he could endure. With something of the spirit of that lord who came to Harry Percy "when the fight was done," he felt that, "but for these vile *gibbets* he would himself have been a *Christian.*" Moderate Christianity he would have readily embraced—Christianity which would have bent before each adverse blast, and gracefully bowed down to idols when Governments or Emperors enjoined it—Christianity without love, without faith, without ardor, above all, without a gleam of that enthusiasm which has always been the bugbear of men of this stamp; and no wonder! for in the long run it drives even their own Divinity, the world, before it.

Guenifoin had two sons, Paul and Constantine, who were Christians; and not "moderate" Christians; there were none such in Japan. Under the sword of persecution there are, alas! for the weakness of man, there always will be, apostates, and may God have mercy upon them; but there is no "moderation" in believing what God has revealed; no "moderation" in obeying His commandments; none of that miserable, nominal religion, which lays no hold on a man's soul. St. Francis Xavier did not cross the ocean, work miracles in the name of Christ, and do in ten years the work of a lifetime, for the sake of teaching his converts to love and to serve God with what the world calls moderation.

The sons of Guenifoin were reckoned amongst the most spirited and accomplished young men of the province of Ximo. From their childhood they had been accustomed to hear their father sneer at the idols and the native priesthood of Japan, and speak with the highest praise of the Christian missionaries. They had often accompanied him to the College of the fathers, and received from them instruction in various branches of learning. Both, when they grew up, became Christians, and, though the Governor of Meaco persisted in ignoring the fact, it was supposed that he did not look upon it altogether with an unfavorable eye. He wished very much to bring about a marriage between Paul, his eldest son, and the daughter of Justo Ucondono; and negotiations on the subject were at that time going on between the two families.

There was to be, the next day, a sort of rehearsal at the palace of Fuximi, in the plain of Ozaca, of the ceremonies to be observed at the reception of the Ambassadors. All the principal personages of the Court and the officers of state were to accompany the Kumbo-Sama on that occasion, and when they separated on the eve of that eventful day most of them felt a little curiosity at the thoughts of witnessing the effect of the colossal building, the forests of pillars, the wide-spread field of gold-fringed cloth, and the luxurious habitations which in the course of a very short time had turned a desert plain into a kind of city of more than ordinary splendor. Even in Justo Ucondono's breast there was, perhaps, a transient feeling of exultation at the thought of the grandeur and the magnificence which his native country would thus display in the eyes of foreigners. It was scarcely possible for a Japanese not to despise the Chinese. The mean, timid, and artful character of that people was singularly repulsive to the chivalrous inhabitants of a small kingdom, which gloried in its independence, and scorned the huge effeminate continental empire which was now suing for peace at their hands.

There was much excitement that night in the streets of Meaco. Preparations for departure were making on all sides; in the palace of the nobles as well as in that of the Kumbo-Sama, a continual noise of footsteps, a hurrying to and fro, and a ceaseless hum of voices was going on. Tradesmen were carrying goods in every direction; wagons loaded with furniture and provisions, and some of them with flowers, so as to look like ambulating gardens, were passing every moment through the gates of the city on their way to Fuximi. The sun set in cloudless majesty that evening, and not a breath of wind stirred the pine forests round the town. The bright stars shone with their steady, placid light on that restless, excited, shifting mass of human life that was thronging the streets and dispersing itself on the plain in anticipation of the glories and the pleasures of the morrow. In the Dairi's palace there was the stolid repose of sensual apathy; of abstraction from human cares enforced and passively submitted to; whilst in the churches of the Jesuits' College and the Franciscan convent the Blessed Sacrament was at that moment exposed, and large numbers of Christians waiting for Benediction. There, too, there was silence—silent prayer, silent hopes, silent fears,—a silence deeper than in the pine forests; holier than in the starry heavens.

But as the Christians emerged from their churches that night, as the workmen prolonged their labors in the palaces and the shops, as the travellers were on their way from Meaco to Fuximi, and darkness had fallen over the busy scene, an extraordinary sight met their eyes as they raised them to the tranquil skies. A blazing meteor of most fearful aspect seemed to cover with its lurid rays the whole of the firmament. It pointed from west to north. There was something so awful in its appearance that not one of those who beheld it could recall, without shuddering, its ghastly color and form; none had ever been seen resembling it. There it stretched across the dark blue expanse, obscuring the stars and threatening the earth. The stoutest heart in Meaco quailed at the sight, and the Chinese portion of the population increased the alarm by raising a dismal cry in the streets of the city.

"Vaza! Vaza!" they shouted in mysterious tones; "an evil omen! an evil omen!"

CHAPTER V.

THE EVE OF THE FESTIVAL.

EVEN as the sun had set in cloudless majesty on the preceding evening, so on the morning of the 30th of August it rose in matchless splendor, and never did its rays illuminate a grander or a brighter scene than Fuximi displayed that day. The Kumbo-Sama was to receive the troops he had assembled, and inspect the buildings he had raised around the wonderful fort, or palace (for the terms are synonymous in Japan), which formed his summer residence. He had built it for the express purpose of immortalizing his name. In order to improve its situation he had levelled huge mountains to the ground, and elevated others at the price of incredible labor. The quaintness of Japanese taste had dealt, in this instance, with mountains, and forests, and rivers, as it was wont to do with the peculiarities of its diminutive gardens—and lately in every direction he had added to the splendor of this Eastern Versailles. One tower amongst many others the Emperor had built for his own use in the centre of the plain, a gigantic pyramid of eight stories high, with spacious galleries, and luxurious apartments richly furnished, and gilt over with incredible magnificence. It was from the highest storey of this edifice that the Ambassadors were to contemplate the vast army encamped in the surrounding plain, and watch its evolutions. Even now, battalion after battalion of well-mounted troops defiled before the gazers from those gilded mansions and lofty towers, till the valley seemed alive with armed men, glittering in the splendor of their gorgeous accoutrements.

A wall of extraordinary thickness, designed at once for ornament and defence, surrounded Fuximi. No enemy that had ever set foot on the soil of Japan could have dreamed of forcing that barrier. In the distance, on a hill, visible from every part of the plain, but not far from Meaco, rose the famous temple of Amida, the sanctuary of the mighty idol Daybut, its white walls glittering in the sunshine, its twelve hundred minor idols each proudly raised on a separate pedestal. Throughout the day, often and often, did Tayco Sama's eyes turn towards that temple, but not to offer homage to the divinities it contained ; no, at those moments he was saying in his heart, like the fool David speaks of, "There is no God." He scorned the gross idolatries of the bonzes, he hated and despised their hypocritical pretences ; he worshipped strength, he worshipped intellect, he worshipped himself ; and this was the moment when that inward worship, which had long been carried on in his secret heart, was to be inaugurated in the face

of day. It was not to rank with the idols of the
bonzes that he cared ; it was not to force Christians
to adhere to the Japanese superstitions that he was
about to set up a new image on their altars. No ;
he did what Voltaire would have wished to do,
what every sceptic would fain accomplish—to drag
down God to his own level by usurping His place
—to enter the list with Him, and by defying His
power to disprove His existence. And all proceeded
according to his desire that day—each building he
had raised was perfect in its kind—each battalion
of his troops passed before him in glorious array.
The whole of that brilliant scene was magical in its
effect—the scarlet draperies and the shrill tones of
the warlike instruments gave a triumphal character to the whole proceedings. A banquet was
spread out on a field of golden cloth, and the
nobles of the land waited on the Kumbo-Sama.
His little son, the heir to all that more than regal
splendor, stood by his side. The Empress and her
attendants were seated in a gallery that overlooked
the gorgeous scene. Everything was fair to the
sight in that hour of luxurious enchantment.
There was nothing to mar the beauty of that
festive hall—no writing on the wall to startle the
serenity of pride, the deep wild joy of successful
ambition. The repast was terminated ; the Emperor rose from his couch of state, and smiled
complacently on his obsequious courtiers, as a
huge chariot appeared in the distance, driven by
twelve magnificently comparisoned white horses,

escorted by a detachment of cavalry, and heralded by a procession of bonzes. He affected to gaze with curiosity on the approach of the triumphal car. The Empress advanced to the edge of the balcony, and inquired of her attendants what was the meaning of that procession.

"It is the statue of the Kumbo-Sama on its way to the Temple of Amida," was the answer. "His gracious Majesty is to judge this day if it is worthy of the homage it is henceforward to receive as the image of our divine Sovereign."

Laurentia, who was standing amongst the attendants, became very pale. She likewise leant over the balcony, at the opposite side from the Empress, in an attitude which betokened intense anxiety.

When the chariot stopped opposite to the place where the Emperor was standing, the bonzes intoned a slow kind of chant; the purple covering was removed, and the statue displayed. The eyes of the Kumbo-Sama fixed themselves upon it. A smile, that almost resembled a sneer, passed over his countenance. It was not under the form of that vain idol that he worshipped himself. What he worshipped was that powerful will he felt within him, and which was about to constrain millions of men to prostrate themselves before his image.

There was no edict published yet. No formal order had been given, but his heathen courtiers fell with their faces on the ground, and the bystanders followed their example, whilst exclamations rent the air, and a flourish of wind instruments resounded on every side.

The Christians stood up silently, respectfully, with their eyes bent on the ground. They stirred not a muscle. They breathed not a word. They held their peace.

Dark grew the brow of the Kumbo-Sama, and rigid the expression of his mouth. He raised his arm and pointed to the Temple of Amida, "To-morrow," he cried, "at the shrine of the mighty Daybut we pay our homage: to-morrow we kneel at the feet of our twelve hundred predecessors ; to-morrow we take our place amongst them." Loud acclamations arose. "To-morrow—"

What checked the words on the lips of the great Emperor? What has startled the prostrate heathens? What strange and horrible sound, like the howling of a fierce wind in the bowels of the earth, has pierced their ears? The sky has become suddenly overcast, a heavy shower of blood-red sand blinds the eyes of the monarch, and causes him to hide his face with the hand a moment ago so proudly uplifted.

"Take the statue to the Temple," he hastily cried, and withdrew into the tower, where the women stood in fear and trembling, listening to those dreadful sounds and watching that strange shower of blistering sand.

The monarch has ascended to the highest storey of his gilded tower. He has summoned his officers of state around him. He has given his orders for the morrow. He has sketched out the ceremonial to be observed in the inauguration of his statue. He has read the edict which is to be published in all the towns of his dominions. He glares on the High Admiral and on Justo Ucondono. He is tired of tolerating the Christians. The fathers have presumed on his patience. The emissaries of the Spaniards, the brown-robed priests, have defied him openly. Let that one true God they are always canting about save them if He can. He would not trust to Him any more than to the divine Cosca or to the mighty Daybut, if he had not his fortress to rely upon. "Show me a God," he cried, "that can baffle my will, and I will believe in Him."

He went towards the gallery. The sky was once more clear; there was not a cloud to be seen; the sand had ceased to fall, but that strange unnatural sound was still going on. He dismissed his officers and counsellors. They withdrew to the lodgings assigned to them in the neighboring palaces. The Empress to the one she occupied opposite the Kumbo-Sama's own residence—that gilded overtowering Babel of matchless grandeur.

The monarch lies down on his splendid couch. He cannot sleep at first, but gradually he falls into an uneasy slumber. He dreams that he has driven the God of the Christians from His home in the skies. He struggles to retain his hold of the golden throne he has won, but it falters under him; it escapes him; it rocks, he is falling with it. He hears a piercing cry, "O Father!" it is his son's voice. He is awake now. Why does everything reel round him? "O Father!" that cry again. He springs to his feet. The tower is rocking, it is swinging to and fro like a drunken man. The noise in his ears is horrible, it sounds like the cries of dying men. He rushes out of his room, he calls upon his attendants, and it seems to him that shouts of derisive laughter answer him. He snatches up his son whom he meets at the door. He descends the winding galleries amidst rattling stones and falling beams. Now, now the earth quakes again, and the last storey he has reached gives way. He falls on the ground, with a mass of ruins heaped over his head. There he lies, the mighty Emperor, the man who has defied God, alone with his child in his arms; alone during the long hours of darkness. When the dawn comes he struggles with the heavy load which weighs him down, and emerges at last from that living tomb which had well-nigh enclosed him for ever. Once more he stands upon his feet, with the sky above him, its pale stars disappearing one by one in the gray dawn of morning. What meets his eyes? One vast universal scene of devastation—yawning crevices, shapeless masses of stone, heaps of shattered columns; torn and soiled fragments of golden cloth and purple drapery hanging, as in mockery, on the disfigured and prostrate ruins; men with pale and haggard faces wandering about carrying dead bodies, or searching for the corpses still buried beneath the remains of those costly buildings now levelled to the ground. It was a horrible sight, and ghastly were the faces both of the living and the dead.

The Emperor shuddered, and stood for a moment as if fascinated by that spectacle of utter desolation. Pride was making wild havoc in his brain. Never had that master passion received a more sudden and violent overthrow. He had defied his Maker. He remembered it well, as he stood there on the same spot where the day before he had so daringly blasphemed, and the challenge had been accepted. He felt himself conquered; words similar to those of the apostate Julian burst from his lips, and he fled from that place with a wild and bitter cry; with his infant son in his arms, like a man pursued by assassins, he fled; the earth was yawning under his feet; every moment dreadful crevices were opening in the solid earth, which seemed endued with life, so fearful were its throes, so loud its subterranean echoes. He rushed towards the hills, and passed in that frantic flight by the Temple of Amida. The wreck there was complete: there was scarcely one stone left on another of that far-famed building—the pride of the Ximo and the glory of Japan. The idol Daybut, and the twelve hundred images, and the statue of the reigning monarch, were all lying on the ground in broken, disfigured, and abject prostration. Several hundred of the bonzes had perished that night; some few left alive were rending the air with cries; but the Imperial fugitive tarried not on his way. The sight of man was torture to him. He could not brook the glance of a human eye; the very beasts of the field as they looked upon him seemed to insult his misery. He fled from the ruined temple as he had fled from Fuximi. The groans of the dying seemed to pursue him as he resumed that desperate and hopeless flight. He thought he heard those words which had re-echoed in the streets of Meaco on the eve of his departure: Vaza! vaza! an evil omen! an evil omen! The howling wind, as he neared the mountain tops, seemed to shout them in his ears. Panting, exhausted with anguish and fatigue, his strength failed him as he reached the highest ridge of Saxuma. He built himself there a hut of rushes and reeds, and hid himself a long time from the sight of his fellow-men. His flight had been traced, and those of his officers who had escaped the horrible disasters of the earthquake went in search of their Sovereign. He was sitting in gloomy silence in the solitary hut—a moody melancholy possessing him. None could summon courage to approach the monarch at bay: not vanquished by an enemy, but maddened by his own pride. "It is a fearful thing to enter the lists with the true God." Many a reckless man felt this in his heart as he thought of that strange night and that stranger morrow.

Guenifoin and Justo Ucondono at last ventured into the presence of the Kumbo-Sama. He looked at them in a bewildered, helpless manner; then he said to the latter, "Your God had reason to be offended with me. I shall manage better another time."

Guenifoin thought from these words he might become a Christian—then he himself would also have been one—but Justo saw nothing in the scowling eye, the lowering brow, the suspicious glance of the Japanese Pharaoh to awaken that hope.

Day after day passed by; weeks and months elapsed; and still the Emperor dwelt on that mountain top, and obstinately refused to return to his duties or his pleasures. It almost seemed as if the grace of conversion had been offered to him then. God had done His part—from the bowels of the earth, as once from the opening sky, a voice had said, "Why persecutest thou Me?" That voice smote the proud man to the ground, but he heeded it not. He lay there awhile in mute helplessness, and then, after a time, he rose up, not to say like St. Paul, "What will Thou have me to do?" but to lift up his arm once more against God and His Christ, and alas! for him, never in this world again to feel the chastening hand of that God.

The earthquake had done its work over the whole face of the Ximo. At Meaco, at Ozaca, at Saccai, as well as at Fuximi, the devastation had been fearful, the loss of life grievous, but marvellously had the Christians been spared. Not one of their churches was destroyed; and it was remarked that the houses where the Holy Sacrifice had been habitually offered, like those of the Israelites in the land of Egypt, seemed to have been marked by the precious blood and saved from destruction. The house which the Empress inhabited at Fuximi on the night of the 30th of August, although it had been greatly shattered, and part of it levelled to the ground, had not been altogether annihilated, and but few lives were lost within its precincts.

Laurentia had not closed her eyes all that night. The earthquake had not taken her by surprise— from the moment that the subterranean sounds had been heard she had felt a presentiment that some great disaster was at hand. She had not gone to bed, but remained on her knees, her face buried in her hands, as if she could find no refuge from a great suffering or a great fear but in the act of ceaseless, ardent prayer. The courageous maiden who had so often given proof of invincible constancy when the periodical persecutions (to which the Christians were ever liable in Japan) had been raging, had grown timid now. There seemed a heavy burden on her heart; and when the fatal catastrophe took place there was an expression of despair in her face which ill agreed with the fearless faith and pious courage which had hitherto marked her character. She rushed out of her apartment and inquired of the attendants who were running about in wild affright, where her brother was. She clung to them with a kind of terrified pertinacity. "My brother," she kept repeating; "My brother Matthias, the painter; tell me, in mercy tell me, where he lodges." No one knew; no one heeded her. She wrung her hands and went out into the darkness, calling on her brother in tones of the deepest anguish. She did not take heed of the yawning chasms; she stumbled over the crumbling ruins; she heard the dreadful cries of the dying, and clasped her hands to her head, as if the anguish of that search was more than she could bear.

The earthquake was over; but the internal convulsions were still going on, and the soil kept opening in different places and forming awful precipices under the wanderer's feet. The darkness increased the danger. As Laurentia was pursuing her hopeless, agonizing search—for such it seemed to be, and she had spent in it several hours of the night—she suddenly felt the ground giving way under her feet, and sank into a pit, from which there appeared no means of escape; she fell against a rock and bruised her head; feeling very faint, she clasped her hands and murmured, "Now, my God, it is all over; I can do no more, I must lie down here and die, but *Thou*, O my God, do Thou save him, save him, save him!" she cried, as if her whole soul was in those words. "Matthias!" she cried again, after a moment's silence, "Matthias!"

"Who is calling me?" answered a voice which thrilled through her heart.

"I am faint and dreaming," thought the maiden. "Where did that voice come from? I have been told that sometimes at the moment of death strange apparitions haunt us; but I want to think only of God and Matthias now."

"Who names Matthias," said the same voice again, and it sounded much nearer than before; "I am here, I am coming."

"Who are you? Where are you?" murmured Laurentia.

"I am here," and now the speaker was quite close to her, and the moon shone out just then between two dark clouds, and its rays fell on a face which was bending over the chasm, as if in search of her. Again she thought it was a delusion, but the name of "Isafai" burst from her lips.

"Laurentia, dear Laurentia, is it you?"

"Isafai," she again faintly said. He had descended into the pit, and was gently raising her from the ground.

"Matthias, where are you?" cried some voices in the distance.

"Oh!" exclaimed Laurentia, with a sort of cry, "they are seeking for him too."

"They are calling *me*, dearest; my Christian name is Matthias."

"Your Christian name, Isafai? O God, I thank Thee—then death has lost its sting. What have I said? Oh, the bewildering joy, the bewildering misery of this hour! Raise me up. Help me to move. Help, help; I must seek him. He *cannot*, cannot have died to-night."

Supported by one she had scarcely hoped ever to see again, Laurentia ascended with trembling steps the side of the precipice which had formed itself under her feet. Isafai's friends were holding torches and throwing light on their way. When they had gained a spot where the footing seemed secure she sank down on the ground exhausted; but clasping her hands, she looked up beseechingly into the faces of those around her, and said, "For God's sake, for mercy's sake, help me to find my brother Matthias."

"Matthias?" said one of the young men, turning towards Isafai.

"Her brother is a Christian, called, like me, Matthias," he said.

"What, the painter of that name?" asked one of the young men.

"Yes," eagerly cried Laurentia; "Matthias, the painter of fans." She listened breathlessly for the next words of the speaker, who was one of the catechists of the recently arrived Franciscan fathers at the Porziuncula Convent.

"An hour or two," he said, "before the news of the catastrophe had reached us, there arrived at the door of our house a man, pale, trembling, and almost fainting with fatigue. He made his way into the chapel, and straight to one of the confessionals. His sobs were audible to me as I stood in the sacristy; they seemed to convulse his whole frame. Maiden, I can see a likeness between his face and yours; as you emerged from that dark pit, and the light fell on your features, it struck me at once that I had lately seen some one very like you, and I now call to mind that it was that poor young man who went to confession to Father Peter Baptiste."

Laurentia's eyes were raised to heaven with intense thankfulness; a fervent "Deo gratias" rose from the very depths of her heart. She did not seem, strange to say, for one moment to doubt that the penitent in the Franciscan church was indeed her brother. Peace, the deep peace of an inexpressible relief, came over her face; but as is often the case when the pressure of an intense anxiety is removed, her physical strength gave way, and she fainted. The little band of Christian brothers carefully removed her to a place of shelter which had been hastily erected in a spot removed from any buildings, and, as far as could be foreseen, safe from present dangers. From thence she returned for a while, with the Empress's permission, to her own home at Meaco.

CHAPTER VI.

THE JAPANESE BRIDES.

LAURENTIA's health had been much affected by the sufferings of that awful night, and for many weeks she was laid on a bed of sickness; but her heart was full of a new joy and a new hope, which made this earth appear almost too bright and beautiful in her eyes. There are few, very few, even of the best amongst us, who are not selfish. It is comparatively easy to sacrifice oneself, to perform acts of self-abnegation, to work for others, and to be careless of one's own comforts; but to live so in others, and feel so keenly for their spiritual and temporal miseries as to lose sight of one's own feelings of joy and sorrow, is a very rare degree of perfection.

Laurentia found the beautiful city of her birth half-levelled with the ground. By a strange dispensation (for it is not often, since Christ came into the world to open and inaugurate the royal road of sorrow, that temporal blessings are vouchsafed as a mark of favor to His servants,) the abodes of the Christians had there, as elsewhere, been preserved from the effects of a calamity which seemed to have been sent as a direct rebuke to the vain glory of

man. Her own little abode stood unscathed amidst
a mass of ruins. The churches of the Jesuits and
of the Franciscans were untouched, though every
temple had been beaten down, and every idol
destroyed. Thousands of the inhabitants of Meaco,
heathens as well as Christians, had instinctively
sought shelter in and around the Christian sanctua-
ries ; and prayers have been said, and litanies sung
during the livelong night as peacefully as if the
murmur of some quiet stream, or the sweet whisper
of the summer breeze, had been accompanying the
solemn chant, instead of the dreadful noise of
falling edifices and reverberating echoes of crumbling fortifications.

There was deep suffering through the city, and
cries of mourning and lamentation over the whole
country; and Laurentia grieved for this wide-
extended desolation, and to relieve it would probably
have given up all she possessed or all she hoped
for in life; but nevertheless there was joy in her
heart, irrepressible, intense, immense joy. "Isafai
had returned, and Isafai was a Christian !" Yes,
during the days she had spent near Fuximi, too ill
to be removed, tended by some Christian women
from Ozaca, and visited by one of the fathers
resident there, she had learnt that he had returned
from Europe a fervent, earnest, devoted Christian.
From his own lips she had heard the history of
his converson: how he had watched day by day
the conduct of his young master, Mancia Ito, and
that of the other ambassadors; their unalterable

patience during the sufferings of a three years' voyage, in which they had experienced every vicissitude which the violence of the elements and the trial of sickness could occasion; how resigned they had been at the prospect of death; how gently submissive to the instructions of Father Valignan, who was at once their guide and their spiritual adviser; how perfectly humble amidst the intoxicating excitement of a journey through Portugal, Spain, and Italy, which had been one long-continued festival. They never neglected their prayers or their studies; they practised every virtue which they had been trained in at home, and maintained recollection amidst the strangest and most seductive change of scene which youths of their age had ever been exposed to.

At Rome he had beheld Gregory XIII. clasping to his breast those youthful envoys from a distant Church, and calling them his children; he had visited with them the old basilicas of the Eternal City, and seen them kneel before the wooden cross of the Colosseum—type of the triumph of Christian humility over the blood-stained pomp of the Roman Empire. He had gazed on that wonderful land, set apart as it were for the spiritual monarchy of the world; akin to the Church by ties which can never be dissevered, which every successive age has made an attempt to unloose, and has ended by riveting; akin to it by the vast, shadowy, spiritual character of its beauty; the solemn impress of sorrow stamped on its loveliness; and the tranquil, soul-subduing serenity of its climate.

He had gone with them into the Catacombs and to the Vatican, and his pride had given way at the feet of that old man, who, whether from those subterranean prisons or from his throne at St. Peter's, reigns with so matchless a power over the hearts and the consciences of men. "And I too will be a Christian," burst from his lips, as he felt that hand extended over his head whose weakness is more powerful than the strength of a combined world.

He had been received into the Church in the sanctuary which bears the sacred name of the Redeemer of mankind, and from whence laborers go forth to the north and to the south, to the east and to the west, bearing that name of power as the symbol of their mission, the pledge of perpetual sufferings and perpetual success—"Through honor and dishonor; through infamy and good name; as seducers and yet speaking the truth; as unknown and yet known." From the moment that Isafai became a Christian, his natural stubbornness of disposition gradually changed into a vigorous firmness of purpose, which can only spring from the soil of a strong character. He applied himself with unwearied perseverance to the correction of his faults, the cultivation of his mind, and the pursuit of virtue.

The affection which had existed between him and Laurentia as children, and developed into a deeper feeling as they advanced in age, which had been made sad and bitter to both by the struggle between her faith on the one side, and his blind

and proud prejudices on the other, now hallowed
by perfect sympathy in religion, in dispositions,
and in tastes, became what love between Christians
should ever be—the most unselfish of friendships,
the strongest stimulus to holiness, the tenderest
upward leading by one soul of another to the point
it has itself reached, and the jealousy of the least
imperfection in the beloved object which may raise
an obstacle between that second self and the God
whom both adore with united hearts and ever-
increasing devotion. No explanations were needed
between them; it seemed so obvious to both, when
they had once met again, and were both Christians,
that their lives were to be spent together, and the
dream of their childhood thus realized, that it did
not occur to them to put into words what neither
for a moment doubted; but they sought the blessing of the fathers and obtained their full approval
of their intended marriage, and Laurentia was
embraced and congratulated by her adopted mother,
Agatha, with more than ordinary tenderness.

She visited her brother at the Franciscan Convent as soon as she was able to go out, for he had
never left it from the time he had fled there on the
evening of the 30th of August. She found him in
the dress worn by the catechists attached to the
Spanish Friars. He had apparently renounced the
world, and Laurentia seemed in no wise surprised
at the change that had come over him.

When they had met for the first time, the hectic
color in his cheek had grown painfully deep, and

he had trembled at her approach. She spoke to him kindly and affectionately, and there was a pensive, humble sort of manner about him that affected her. He begged that she would communicate to the governor of the Empress's household, that even if the late events had not caused the discharge of all her supernumerary attendants, as he understood was the case, that his state of health would incapacitate him from resuming his position at Court. He could not paint; his hands trembled when he attempted it; his occupation was gone, his ambition passed away. The Franciscan Fathers had consented to let him hide himself in the shelter of their house, and he did them whatever services he could; he instructed the converts and visited the sick, and he hoped to remain there all his life.

When Laurentia told him of Isafai's return, of his conversion, and her intended marriage with him, he said, with tears in his eyes, "God be praised for it; you will have in him a good Christian husband. Your natures have been cast in the same mould. God has given you both the gift of strength—bless Him every day for it."

Laurentia threw her arms round his neck, and both wept long and bitterly. "Then Isafai has the same name as I have," he said at last, trying to smile.

"Yes; he chose it he says in remembrance of you, and of the pains you had taken to make him a Christian."

"Did I? Yes; I remember, I often spoke to him on the subject. Well, it is the name of an Apostle, he could not do amiss in choosing it but— However, that is not to the purpose. Where are you to live when you are married?"

"In Nangazaqui, the Christian city. The noble Mancia Ito, when he gave up his possessions and riches to enter the noviciate of the Jesuit Fathers, made some generous presents to Isafai, in return for his devoted services during their long voyage. He has given him a house near the port of Nangazaqui, close to the one which he hopes before long that the holy women from Europe will inhabit. He has told me so much of their pious lives, their ceaseless prayers, their devotion to all good works. It will indeed be a blessed thing for Japan when they set foot on its soil. Think of the joy of ministering to their wants, of sharing their labors. Isafai has some glorious plans for the advancement of religion in our poor country; you must help us with your prayers," she added. A sad and troubled expression passed over her brother's face.

"I!" he cried, "I help you! Sister, do not mock me. Oh! how deeply you must despise me!"

"Hush, hush! Matthias, do not speak so, my dear, dear brother; it was a moment's weakness, an indeliberate act."

"If I could only believe that, I should be stronger another time. If I did not feel that fatal, horrible weakness at my very heart's core. The trial was slight compared to what others have had to endure. Oh, Laurentia, I despair of myself. It was but the other day that I wished to do public penance in the church for my sin, and I asked Father Baptiste for permission to do so. He looked at me a moment, and then said, 'My child, you do not really wish it; do not attempt more than God requires of you.' His words and his looks were kind, but they cut me to the heart. He had read my inmost soul. No sooner had I made my petition than my frame began to tremble and my heart to falter; it is a dreadful trial."

Laurentia wept in silence and then looked up to him earnestly and tenderly. "Brother, it may be that this peculiar and great trial, this intense humiliation, has been sent to you for a special purpose, to sanctify you in a way most trying to nature, most humbling to pride. Depend upon it that God, our good God, will never forsake you if you put your trust in Him. Dearest brother," she gently added, "you were not so sorrowful, not so desponding, the last time we spoke together, and ah, how much safer you are now than you were then! Be sure, be sure, that as you now feel, God will never send you a trial too hard for your strength."

Matthias sighed deeply, and they parted. As she was walking away from the convent, a boy of five or six years old came running up to her with bounding steps and joyous face.

"Have you seen," he cried, "Anselm the musician? I hear he is in town, and I want him so much to play me a tune on his flute. Where do you think he is?"

"I don't know," said Laurentia smiling; "I have not seen him yet; but who are you, my child?"

"I am Augustine."

"Whose son are you?"

"My blessed mother Mary's son," answered the child with a bright smile.

"And where do you live?"

"Why at the College, of course."

"Then what are you doing here?"

"I am going to play with Anthony and Lewis, the acolytes of the new church. Brother Paul Michi brought me here just now, but I remained at the door looking out for Anselm."

"How comes it that you live at the College? What is your business there?"

"I learn my lessons, and I serve the Rector's Mass, and I run messages for the brothers. I think brother John Gotto would go out of his mind sometimes, if I did not help him to light the candles and to gather flowers for the altar."

"No doubt you are a very useful personage," said Laurentia, laughing; "but how long have you been in the convent?"

"How long? I think the fathers say I am almost six years old."

"And you have no father then?"

"God is my father," answered the child, looking reverently up to heaven.

"But, lady, I must not stay here too long, for at four o'clock we are to go back to the College. Our confraternity meets to-day."

"What confraternity? what is it called?" Laurentia asked, more and more interested by the boy's countenance and manner.

"The Children's confraternity of Martyrs," answered the child. "Francis Ucondono is our president; and Lewis and Anthony are our secretaries; and the sons of the Princess Justa, and almost all the Christian little boys in Meaco, belong to it, and I am the treasurer."

"What are your rules?" asked Laurentia. She belonged herself, like almost all the Christians of Japan, to a confraternity of martyrs, who observed a rule of life, and met at certain times with a view to prepare themselves for death in the cause of Christ, but she did not know that the children had banded themselves together for the same purpose.

Augustine explained to her their childish practices of devotion, and showed her the bag in which he collected the contributions of the infant members. "Brother Paul Michi," he said, "took care to send their money to the poor sick and banished Christians.—O Lady," he added, "we sit and tell each other such beautiful stories about all the little children who die for Christ; and we go without our dinners once a week, and we pray every day for five minutes before the Blessed Sacrament that we may be martyrs, and not cry when we are put to death, and if any of us have been naughty we kneel down before all the others and say an Our Father and a Hail Mary."

"Say one Hail Mary for me," said Laurentia, stooping to kiss the boy's fair brow, as she parted from him.

There was something singularly noble and engaging in the countenance and manners of this little boy, and a sudden thought passed across Laurentia's mind—she thought of the story which Grace Ucondono had related the last day they had met at Agatha's house, and she wondered if this might possibly be the child whom the itinerant musician, Anselm, had rescued from a watery grave.

Instead of returning home, she went straight to the palace of Justo Ucondono, and asked to see Grace. She found her engaged in making preparations for a journey, but she suspended her occupation in order to lead her into the garden, where the two friends sat down together in a summer-house, and held a long conversation, in which they opened their hearts to each other on various subjects of the deepest interest. Since they had met, both had become affianced wives: for Grace's marriage to Paul, the eldest son of Guenifoin, had been arranged, and she had willingly acquiesced in the consent which her father had given to the Governor's proposal; for Paul was a fervent Christian, and as a matron she hoped to devote herself with more efficiency, if not with more zeal, than as a maiden, to the interests of the Church and the service of the poor. She knew that her intended husband, like herself, had been thoroughly trained in the principles which teach us to consider ourselves as *servants;* to look upon the *service* of God as the one business of life—the sole purpose of our creation. He was also brave, generous, and kind; one that a Christian woman might look up to with love and respect. It seemed to her God's will that she should marry him, and with many prayers and redoubled acts of humility and charity she was preparing for that great change in her state of life. The news of Isafai's conversion filled her with joy, and the two friends rejoiced together with hearts overflowing with affection and hope. They indulged in bright visions, and spoke of the future as young people do, even when their souls are chastened by deep and holy thoughts. They described to each other what the course of their lives was to be. Laurentia spoke of the house in Nangazaqui, with its turreted roof and its three-storied gallery, overlooking the sea; of the way in which she would sit and watch the approach of the ships which would bear the holy sisterhood to their shores, of the barks laden with merchandise, which Isafai (for she had never yet learned to call him Matthias) was to trade in, and make a fortune, which would enable him to build a small church, such as he had seen in Europe in sea-port towns, dedicated to "Our Lady, Star of the Sea." This was *her* dream. And Grace had also beautiful projects, for her future husband had large possessions, and she would build homes for the abandoned children, and be a mother to them herself; she would have a hospital, where, like St. Elizabeth of Hungary, she might tend the sick with her own hands; and who could tell but that as Paul was very rich they might not raise a splendid church, such as had never before been seen in Japan.

"Oh, yes!" exclaimed Laurentia eagerly, "I will send you the pictures Isafai has brought home of St. Peter's at Rome, and St. Charles at Milan, and Our Lady of the Angels at some other place, and other beautiful ones in Spain and Portugal. And you will call yours 'St. Paul's.'" A bright smile flashed over Grace's face, and Laurentia laughed with delight because the thought was such a joy, and her heart was overflowing with happiness. Poor children, they were indulging in dreams; but not unblessed, nor unhallowed either. If never destined to be realized, they were doubtless the foreshadowings of even higher and better offerings which they were one day to make.

"Laurentia," said Grace, after a pause, during which both had been plucking flowers and scattering them on the grass around them; "Laurentia, we must not set our hearts even on such hopes as these. We must not forget that *suffering* is the best part of a Christian's lot."

"Oh, but we may marry; you, Paul Sacondono, and I, Isafai; and suffer a great deal too," cried Laurentia eagerly.

Grace smiled. "Perhaps so, though at this

moment nothing might seem to us hard to bear but to give up that particular form of happiness which our hearts are set upon. But, dear friend, whose soul and mine have been so long closely united, will you join with me in one prayer before we part? Will you come with me and kneel down before the crucifix in yonder little oratory, and offer to God the sacrifice of our projects and of our hopes if we might serve Him better in any other way, or if the souls of those we love might be more safely directed to heaven under other companionship than ours?"

Tears started in Laurentia's eyes; but she said, "Lead the way, beloved Grace, lead the way, as you have ever done in that upward path in which, but for your example and help, I should so often have lagged behind."

The two maidens knelt before the image of their dying Lord, and made to His Sacred Heart the full and entire sacrifice of all earthly happiness if He should make known to them His will that they should surrender it for His sake. When they rose from their knees they embraced each other, and walked in the sunshine, and amidst the bright flowers and the shining golden fruit, and all the loveliness of earth and sky, with a yet sweeter serenity, a still more divine joy.

Then Grace told her friend that she was about to return for a short time to the Court of the King of Arima.

"Not to that dreadful place," exclaimed Laurentia, "where, if report speaks truly, your life was but lately in danger."

"Circumstances are altogether altered," Grace answered, "and there is not now the slightest shadow of peril for me there, at least not more peril than we Christians live in every day and every hour in our homes in Meaco, at Ozaca, everywhere. The allied Kings have surrendered all their arms, and their troops are disbanded; the contest is at an end, and the disasters of the late earthquake will long prevent its being resumed on either side. My father was at first much opposed to my going there; my mother wept bitterly, and implored him to refuse his consent. Her sorrow grieved me to the heart, but he sees there is no more danger for me now at Arima than at Meaco, and he feels that the salvation of many souls (alas! the weak instruments that God sometimes makes use of to show forth His power) may, humanly speaking, depend upon this visit. My sweet mother has made the sacrifice also, which indeed to her is great, for she cannot repress her fears, groundless as they are. Her Francis goes not with me this time. Oh, if there *was* danger, which there is not, how gladly would I face it, for the sake of but one soul, and in this case I hope—oh, I hope for many, through Father Francis's intercession."

"But what says Paul Sacondono?"

"Paul is not aware of the dangers we ran some time ago, or of what my poor father then endured; but he would not stop me from going where there is work to do for God."

"Before I leave you," said Laurentia, "I wish to tell you of a child who lives at the fathers' College. He is between five and six years of age, very handsome, with much wit and readiness of speech. He has been there ever since he can remember, and is conscious of no parents. Can he by chance be the babe old Anselm found by the river side?"

"He is not blind, of course?" Grace eagerly inquired.

"Oh, no, he has the finest eyes in the world, and seems to make good use of them."

Grace shook her head. "I care not to hear more about him then; he is safe, happy little fellow! We need not trouble ourselves on his account. But when you see Anselm do not forget, dear Laurentia, to speak to him of the child he rescued on the banks of the river near Arima, and ask him this question, was *that* child blind?"

The friends then parted, with many tender farewell words and many affectionate embraces, but it was some time before Grace was enabled to accomplish her intended visit to Arima. Her grandfather, the pious and venerable old man whom she so tenderly loved, died soon after her interview with Laurentia. This occasioned her marriage to be put off for some time; and after spending a few weeks at Tagacuqui with her parents, she proceeded to that city and palace where she had suffered so much, but where a strong and deep interest was now inducing her to return.

CHAPTER VII.

A CONVERSION.

THE Queen of Arima was one of those persons naturally inclined to virtue, and endowed with no common intellectual gifts. She had been married at a very early age to King Fondasadono, a man of violent and capricious temper, and had had much to suffer at his hands, although he was passionately attached to her.

From early youth he and Justo Ucondono had been intimate friends, and neither the difference in their characters nor in their religion had severed that tie. They used often to visit each other, and the King of Arima took a sort of intellectual pleasure in discussing the dogmas of the Christian religion, and making himself acquainted with its practices, although he was not in the least degree inclined to give up his sins and his pleasures in compliance with its laws. He did not know how many Christians in Europe bear that holy name and dishonor it by shameless iniquities. Alas! in those countries where a newly-planted Christian community is displaying the virtues of the primitive Church, the missionaries have no heavier trial than when their neophytes become acquainted with men from the civilized portions of the world whose conduct is utterly at variance with their creed. They cannot understand how a person can be a baptized Christian and wilfully offend the God whom he believes died for him. And Fondasadono himself never dreamed of embracing the Christian religion without renouncing the indulgence of his passions, and that he was determined not to do, but it was a subject of conversation which interested him. He liked to surprise both the Christians and the bonzes by his acquaintance with the tenets of the Catholic religion, by his knowledge of the Holy Scriptures; the practical beauties of which he fully appreciated; by the acuteness and eloquence with which he defeated the arguments of the heathens and denounced the errors of idol worship.

Justo Ucondono was always looking forward to his conversion, and lost no opportunity of urging upon him the duty of availing himself of the means of salvation with which he had so long trifled. Fondasadono made evasive answers; put him off to another season, and went on as before, making an amusement of controversy, and the truths of religion a theme on which to exercise his powers of language. There was nothing he liked better than to repeat to his wife what he had heard from Justo on the subject of his faith; to converse with her was his delight.

She was a woman of extraordinary beauty, and no less remarkable talent. His jealousy had been so keen that from the moment he married her nothing could exceed the precautions he took to keep her in complete seclusion; surrounded indeed with companions and attendants of her own sex, and in the midst of luxuries of every sort, but far from the eyes of men. She had submitted not unwillingly to these restraints. Her mind was keenly active, and she had devoted herself to study and to literary pursuits with an energy not altogether unprecedented, but rare amongst the women of Japan. She drunk in with an eager intellectual thirst, in the first instance, and then by degrees, with an interest ever deeper and deeper, what her husband told her of the Christian faith. There were many persons of that religion in Arima, although there had not for some time been any resident priest there. She had heard of their goodness, and felt an intense curiosity about their worship. Often and often with a woman's skill she would excite her husband to revert to that topic which seemed equally to interest them both, but in how different a manner! He liked to descant on the puerile tenets of the bonzes, and sneer at their immoralities with self-complacent pride at his own acuteness, and a cynical contempt of their pretences to virtue. She listened with an aching heart and an inward shudder to his clever descriptions of the infatuations of their followers, and the misery of their dupes. He spoke of the consistency, of the sublimity, the loveliness of Christian dogmas, and listened to his own well-flowing sentences with a

self-applauding satisfaction. She hearkened with
a beating heart, an eager eye, and a sense of truths
deeper, higher, sweeter than her mind had ever
reached to; a presentiment of some awful mystery
about to be unfolded to her yearning spirit. And
when he read to her the holy poems of the Bible,
of which Justo had given him the translation made
by one of the Jesuit fathers, the fifty-third chapter
of Isaiah, or the lament of David for Jonathan,
the stories of Joseph and of Ruth, or the gospel
narrative, or the burning words of St. Paul, his
eyes gleamed with the light of intellectual pleasure,
hers with the brightness of dawning faith.

There had been a dark and dreadful passage in
that woman's life: the hour when, having given
birth to a child, that child was found to be born
blind. Passionate was the rage and disappointment in Fondasadono's breast when his joy at the
birth of an heir to his throne was thus suddenly
turned to disappointment. The babe was doomed
to death. The mother had submitted to the sentence as people submit to what they have never
deemed it possible to resist, the absolute volitions
of irresponsible power, sanctioned by custom, un-
condemned by public opinion. But since that day
there had seldom been a smile on her lips, and
always a hectic spot on her cheek. Beautiful she
always was; but now and then there was a wild
look in her eye, flashing on its depths of shadowy
beauty like lightning on a dark sky. It was then
that she began more intensely to long to become

acquainted with the God and the faith of the Christians; she had heard something about those who mourned being blessed. It was such a strange sentence. Oh! did she not on the contrary feel as if those who mourn were utterly unblest? Had not that little being she had clasped one moment in her arms and never again beheld, had it not been cursed with a bitter curse, and cast away because a dark shadow had rested on its infant existence? And yet those words rang in her ears, "Blessed are they that mourn." And she had once seen a picture of a Divine Mother holding in her arms her dead Son and saying, "Was there ever sorrow like unto my sorrow?" and she knew that that mother held a place in the heart of Christians by right of that sorrow, which was a sacred one to them. She yearned to know more. Love and faith were slowly expanding in that as yet untaught but instinctively Christian heart.

Then came the last visit of Justo to the Court of Arima, and with him his bright-eyed children. The days passed in rejoicings, and the tournament came off with splendor, and the feasts and the banquets were worthy of Fondasadono's magnificent hospitality. At last the friend of the King's youth took his departure, and left his children behind. Grace had told how the Queen was ever seeking to gain from her information about the true religion, and that they knelt together every day, unseen by any one in the palace, and repeated the prayers of the Church. Then, like a dark cloud overcasting the horizon, came the rebellion of the six allied princes, and the passions of men raged with a violence which knew no limits. Fondasadono was a weak as well as a violent man. That unhappy combination of defects is, unfortunately, not a rare one. His interests were bound up with those of his more powerful neighbors, and the dilemma in which he found himself increased his fury against his friend. He was angry with him for the conflict which was torturing his own soul.

> "And to be wroth with one we love,
> Doth work like madness in the brain."

He suffered dreadfully himself at the part he took about Justo's children, and, as has been said in a former chapter, when a favorable opportunity occurred he connived at their escape; when peace was re-established, he sought a reconciliation with Justo, and offered, if he would forgive his past conduct, to invite the missionaries to Arima and allow them the free exercise of their religion. The proposal was readily accepted, for the Christians of that city had long been pining for the return of their pastors; and the church and house which they had formerly occupied was speedily prepared for their reception. Father Cespedes was sent to this mission, and took with him Vincent, a Japanese brother of his order, who was remarkable for his talent in preaching.

The King, as usual, took pleasure in hearing his discourses, and was wont to repeat portions of them to the Queen. She intensely desired to hear herself these sermons, but she knew that it would be in vain to ask her husband's permission. The close imprisonment, though in a most beautiful place of confinement, in which he had kept her all her married life, he never intended to relax. The least mention of the subject threw him into paroxysms of passion.

It was at this time she wrote to implore Grace to come to her. In addition to the invitation, which was given with the customary formalities, she had taken occasion to send her, by old Matthew the comb-seller, who had one day been admitted with his stock of merchandise into the palace at Arima, a letter, in which she described to her her position and the great need she had of her company and assistance. Her husband joined his persuasions to hers, for, although he was beginning to suspect his wife of a leaning towards the Christian religion, which with a strange inconsistency he was determined to repress in the severest manner, he was anxious to show civility to his friend's daughter, and to efface the memory of the painful events connected with her last residence at his Court.

The meeting between Grace and the Queen was touching in the extreme; they shed tears of sorrow and of joy as they held each other in close embrace; and the deeply tried woman poured forth her anxieties, her doubts, and her trials, in the ear of the young and happy being who seemed to her like an angel sent to her deliverance. She related to her how a few days previously she had consulted her ladies as to the possibility of visiting the Christian church. They were all of them devoted to her; and since the time of Grace's visit such had been the effect of her words, of her example, and above all of that intrepid courage which she and her young brother had shown in the presence of the most awful danger, that they had become strongly inclined to share the Queen's scarcely concealed inclination towards the Christian religion; but they represented to her, with justice, that it would be impossible to pass through the guards at the palace gate, who had received orders not to let her Majesty go beyond them on any pretext whatever. If, indeed, unattended but by two or three of her ladies, she would venture out at the back door of the palace, of which they possessed the keys, it might be possible thus to accomplish her design. Accordingly, on a day when the heathens were wont to visit their temples, and at the hour when most of them were thronged with worshippers, the Queen stole out privately in disguise and went straight to the father's church.

"It is difficult," she said, clasping Grace's hand, "to describe to you what I felt on entering that sacred edifice. At the first moment, as if by an unerring instinct, I fell on my knees and touched the stones with my forehead. I *felt* God's presence there—that God," she said, lifting her dark troubled eyes to heaven, "whom I believe in, though His servant has refused to make me His child; I cannot say yet, 'Our Father,' Grace; I am still unbaptized."

"God is your creator, in that sense your Father, beloved lady; and if you long for baptism you are already very near His Sacred Heart."

"Well, I remained prostrate for some instants, and then I raised my eyes, and saw above me, over the altar, the Christian altar, that Divine image which I had so often pictured to myself of Christ crucified, God dying. Your little crucifix, you know, I had often gazed at; but this picture was so life-like; it has remained before my eyes ever since; I seem to see it wherever I go; I could have looked at it for hours, but some one came up to me and desired to know my commands. It was one of your fathers, Grace, one of the servants of Jesus. There was such majesty on his brow, such kindness in his voice, that I trembled. I had never done so in my life before, but it was so new to be addressed by one very humble in manner but yet who spoke as having authority. I told him I was come to hear the sermon. The preacher, Brother Vincent, was not yet arrived; in the meantime I was shown the church. It seemed as if I was dreaming. I had often dreamed of going into a Christian church, and now this was the reality. Everything I saw and everything that was said to me seemed to fill up a void in my heart, and to satisfy the secret yearnings of my soul. At last Brother Vincent returned, and he preached. Oh, Grace! That Christian sermon! The first I ever heard; it may be the last that I shall ever hear; how every word of it remained stamped on my mind, as if written there in letters of light! It was sweet, yet very awful; some doubts I still had, some things were yet dark to me; but it was as a mist hanging on the side of a mountain and obscuring some portion of the landscape even whilst the glorious sun illumines the rest—there is darkness here and there, but we feel it is about to pass away. When Brother Vincent—you know he is a Japanese, Grace, a countryman of ours—had finished his discourse, I went to him, in a little adjoining room where the church ornaments are kept, and asked him some questions. He gave me answers which satisfied many of my doubts, though he could not explain to me everything at once. Then with earnest prayers and tears, for my heart was very full, I implored him to baptize me, and I think he wished to do so, but the father I was speaking of—"

"Father Cespedes," said Grace with a smile.

"Ah! you know him then? He is one to fear as well as to love; but those who have once spoken with him would never, I think, forget his words; I never can, though God knows if I shall ever speak again to him, or to any Christian priest. He would not suffer me to be baptized. He said it could not be. I wept bitterly, and answered, what was too true, that I might never again, as long as I lived, be able to return; and something too I added about the King, but not enough to make him understand who I was; for I have since heard that he supposed

me to be one of Fondasadono's three hundred
wives, but not the Queen. Till he knew more
about me, he said, it was impossible that I could
be baptized. It was necessary to be instructed and
prepared for the reception of that sacrament. I
had not the presence of mind to explain to him how
long it was since I had desired it; and could only
repeat in a hurried manner, that if he did not take
advantage of this opportunity to receive me into
the Church he might never see me again. Alas!
at that moment a number of the King's guards
appeared at the door of the sacred building, and
told me that I had been missed at the palace, and
that a palanquin had been sent for me. They had
vainly inquired for the Queen at all the temples,
and at last bethought themselves of seeking her at
the Christian church. Since that day, dearest
Grace, the doors of this royal prison have closed
upon me with inexorable rigor; but my ladies and
my dear maids, like messenger birds betwixt earth
and heaven, have gone constantly backwards and
forwards from the palace to the church; they carry
from me to the father questions which I write
down, and bring me back the answers. Seventeen
of them have obtained the blessing which their
poor Queen is languishing for; they are Christians
now, baptized children of Jesus. Of late, some
constraint has been put upon them by the King's
orders; but a gentleman of the Court carried a
message from one of them to Brother Vincent, and
that very hour his heart was touched by the grace

which works such strange wonders at this moment in so many souls, and within the last few days he too has abjured the worship of idols and embraced the true religion. Now, sweet Grace, is not your poor friend to be pitied, who sees her companions and her servants seeking and finding the pure fountain of life, and is doomed to gaze from a distance on the bright waters, whilst a burning thirst consumes her soul?"

"To purify, to refine, to strengthen it, beloved Queen," was Grace's reply; "God has ways of compassing His designs which we little foresee. Patience and courage; those are the words you have long known the meaning of. Faith and charity are Christian words, which you will soon grow familiar with, and soon you will learn to love as well as to endure suffering."

In such conversations as these the first days of Grace's residence in the palace of Arima were spent. But the King wished her to be entertained with every courteous demonstration of regard and affection. Theatrical representations were got up, and concerts performed, to afford her amusement; but everything of the kind took place within the walls of the palace. She had of course free egress from it to the town, and each day she went to the church and conferred with the fathers, who enjoyed for the moment a considerable amount of freedom in the exercise of their religion. Through her they advised the Queen as to her mode of life; and with her Christian attendants and her young visitor she observed every holy day, she practised every devotional observance in her power, and became every day more imbued with the spirit of the Christian faith.

One evening the King had ordered that the best musicians in the town should be assembled to give the Queen and her ladies the surprise of a serenade in the gardens of the palace. They had been playing some time when one of them informed the governor of the household that there was at that moment in Arima a poor man who played most beautifully on the flute. It was strange, he added, that so rare a talent should exist in one who had never, it seemed, risen above the state of poverty, and who wandered about the country as an itinerant musician. One of the ladies was desired to ask the Queen if it would please her Majesty that the flute-player be summoned to perform in her presence one of his exquisite pieces of music.

"Say yes," whispered Grace, whose heart was beating with a strong hope which was destined to be realized, for it was old Anselm, the Christian stroller through plains and through cities, who had made his way to Arima, and who was now ushered into the royal presence.

He stood before that group of noble ladies and maidens, and his aged eyes filled with tears of joy, for he had heard that they were almost all of them Christians, and that the pale beautiful Queen who sat amongst them was a catechumen. He played some of the chants of the Christian churches; the solemn sweet notes of the "Stabat Mater," varied with a simple skill and a deep pathos, which seemed to speak the very words of that song of matchless sorrow; then the joyous tones of the "Adeste Fideles" floated on the breeze, and gladdend the ears of Grace, who knew the Christian meaning of its summons to rejoice.

The playing of the old man was beautiful, but when Grace had whispered to the Queen that he was a Christian, she greatly desired to converse with him. He had seen and known St. Francis Xavier, and witnessed the beginning of the Church of Japan. It was a theme on which he could speak with the eloquence of the heart. He described the saint, his ascetic appearance, his wonderful simplicity, his supernatural gifts, till the hearts of those who heard him began to glow with an unwonted fervor. They wearied not of listening to his accounts of the great Apostle of the Indies. The Queen hung enraptured on his words.

"Ay," continued the old man, with a beaming smile, "and he to whom Almighty God gave such power whilst he lived on this poor earth has power in heaven also; there is scarcely a year passes that some miracle wrought by his intercession does not gladden the Christians, and confirm their faith and their hope. It was but a few months ago that, at the college of the fathers at Meaco, the application of a handkerchief which had belonged to him to the eyes of a child born blind restored him to sight."

The Queen breathed one of those deep sighs

which rise from the heart where a sorrow lies deeply buried, and is touched by unconscious words at random spoken. The color rushed into Grace's cheeks, she half started from her seat, and then sat down again, commanding herself to be patient and prudent. It was a difficult matter ; she could hardly brook the delay ; but to give one ray of hope to her friend, to raise in her mind the thought of a possibility beyond the wildest dream of happiness which her imagination could have pictured, she felt would be a fearfully cruel act ; but she must speak to Anselm ; she must tell him that night that the following day they must meet at the church.

After he had played once more the "Stabat Mater" at the Queen's request, Grace contrived to make the appointment with him ; and then taking notice of the dark, troubled look in the Queen's face, which always followed upon any allusion to the subject which so deeply agitated her, and to beguile also her own anxious thoughts from that too engrossing theme, she called upon Anselm to relate one of those stories of Christian suffering and Christian heroism which he had witnessed in the course of his long and chequered life. She knew that he was a poet as well as a musician, and that his language grew eloquent when he spoke of the apostles, the heroes, and the victims of his faith.

"Do, good Anselm," she said, "do tell the Queen and these ladies a tale of Omura, or of Goto, of the holy King Bartholomew, the noble

Sumitando, of Sebastian, or Lewis, or the young Prince Simon, your beloved Chicatora."

Anselm answered with a smile, "The old man will weary his kind listeners if he once begins to speak of those he has loved in his youth; of those holy Christian princes and their friends and teachers, Father Cosmas de Torres, Father Cabral, and that great and good servant of God, Father Valignan."

"Oh no, good Anselm," said the Queen, "we also love the names which are so dear to you."

The aged flute-player mused for awhile in silence, and raised his eyes to heaven. God had endowed him with gifts which he had never used but for His glory, and he therefore confidently asked His help whenever he was about to exert them in His cause. Prayer was the talisman which he used to reach the hearts of his hearers even whilst eloquent words flowed from his lips or the notes of his instrument vibrated in their ears. He looked on that pensive heathen Queen, even then standing on the threshold of the Church, and that group of young and untried converts around her, and whilst preparing to speak before them of the trials others had endured for their faith, he prayed that his words might impart strength to their souls.

"Mine," he began, "has been a wandering existence; I have witnessed many extraordinary scenes, and looked upon faces which I shall never behold again until we all stand at God's judgment seat. I have seen Sumitando break with his powerful arm the idol Mantiffen, and brave the fury of a thousand indignant bonzes. I have seen Prince Lewis ride to the Christian church in Goto, and when the edict against the Christians was proclaimed, stand in the porch with a cross in his hand, encouraging by word and gesture the crowds that flocked to martyrdom. I could tell you of the virtues of the good King Francis, and of the poverty of the holy Catherine, who gave away all her great riches, and converted numbers to the faith. But there is one form, one countenance, one image, which can never pass away from my memory as long as age does not obliterate from its tablet every trace of the past.

"When first I beheld the young Prince Chicatora, life was lying before him as a plain undarkened by the shadow of a cloud, or a smooth sea unrippled by a wave. The brother-in-law of the King of Bungo, the brave and wise Cicatondono, had adopted him, and loved the son of his choice with a passionate affection. His sister, the proud Queen (whom our people called the Jezebel of Japan), the most beautiful of the women of her time, was his protectress; and her daughter, the loveliest rosebud that ever blossomed in a courtly garden, his affianced bride. But he had heard of the one true God whom the Christians adored; he received the teachings of the Christian faith, he believed, and for ever foreswore the idol worship of his country. Then the struggle began. The more he was

*12

beloved, the more his religion was hated, it stood like an enemy between his kindred and him. Fierce, desperate, reckless, was the war they waged against it. No means were left untried; neither the impassioned pleadings of parental affection, nor the cunning schemes of an artful policy, nor the smiles of woman, nor the blandishments of praise, nor the seductions of pleasure. It was an unequal combat, if truth had not been on his side. The Queen was a woman of strong will, wonderful intellect, relentless perseverance. Never in any human eyes have I seen such an expression as in hers: it would have been fine if it had not been fearful. When she was pleased it was like the lightning playing on a dark cloud; but when anger caused those eyes to flash, nothing in nature can be compared to that hateful gleam, unless the glance of a wild beast about to dart on its prey.

"It would be too long to tell with what wiles, with what arts, with what violence, with what fury she drove her brother to persecute his adopted son, and her husband, the king (who even at that time was half a Christian himself) to permit this ill-usage.

"I saw him, this young prince—not yet baptized, but a Christian in heart—shut up in a loathsome dungeon; where, in despite of the love he bore him, his father had suffered him to be confined, and deprived of the very necessaries of life, in the hopes of shaking his faith. Month after month he languished there, forbidden to see or to speak with a Christian; daily tormented with threats, and deceived by false communications artfully conveyed. But one day that he was ill, his guards became anxious for his life, and the flute-player, who had long and anxiously hovered around those walls, was summoned into the tower, and desired to raise the prince's spirits by the music which he loved. I was admitted into his presence, and I can see his beautiful face even now—pale and dejected, but the very image of patient suffering—as he looked kindly upon me, whilst I knelt by the side of his couch. 'Anselm,' he whispered, for he had often noticed me in past years, when I played on the flute in the streets, 'Anselm, we must not converse, or they will hurry you away. But one word I must say whilst you are tuning your instrument. I can bear everything but what I have lately suffered. I know you are a Christian. For the love of Christ, go to Father Organtin, and ask him if he did indeed send me word that for the sake of the Church, and to save the lives of Christians, I must disguise my faith and profess myself a heathen. If he commands me to do so, I must obey; but they are deceiving me, perhaps, and I think God has sent you to my aid to clear up this dreadful doubt. You will find means of letting me know his answer. Now begin to play, or my guards will dismiss you.'

"The next time I saw the Prince was at a great tournament in the plain of Vosuqui. He was magnificently dressed, and seated in the midst of the royal family; the most beautiful women of the Court were around him. The Queen with her basilisk eyes watching him with an expression in which affection and hatred seemed combined, like in the caress of a tiger or the blandishments of a vulture. Melodious strains were floating in the air; gorgeous banners proudly waving in the wind; worldly pomp and grandeur compassing him about on every side, but his face was almost as pale as in the prison; his eyes were wandering anxiously over the assembled crowd. That eager glance met mine. It was enough. The color rushed to his cheek; he rose and advanced slowly, as if by accident, towards the spot where I stood. I gave him a letter from Father Organtin. The next instant the crowd had separated us, and I saw him no more that day. A few hours later the palace and the whole city were in an uproar. The King was absent, but the Queen and her brother Cicatondono had issued a proclamation threatening the Christians with death. The festival was at an end. The palace wrapped up in sadness and gloom; the Queen raving, it was said, and the bonzes vainly striving by their incantations to lay the demon her wild passions had evoked.

"Cicatora had walked straight from the tournament to the church and been baptized; he received the name of Simon, and returned to the palace, his face beaming with a joy so celestial that it struck all who beheld him. In the presence of the assembled Court he proclaimed the faith which he had awhile disguised, and by the burning eloquence of his avowal made several converts on the spot. Wild was the Queen's fury, and fierce her threats against the priests. But even as she was preparing an edict against the Christians, and loading her nephew with chains, her own son, Prince Sebastian, was riding to the church with all the Christian nobles of the town, and drawing their swords to defend the servants of God; but the fathers compelled them to lay down their arms, and instead of fighting to kneel down and pray. Never shall I forget the expression of these young warriors' faces as they laid down their arms before the altar, the self-conquest of that hour, the triumph of that submission, nor the divine smile with which Cicatora received the order to return to his dungeon and await his fate. But he was not doomed to linger for ever in confinement, nor to pine away his life in slow decay. Another and more glorious doom was awaiting him. He was sent for to Court again. Once more tempted, once again surrounded with every allurement that can be offered to the weakness of youth and the passions of manhood, and he stood firm, and, by God's grace, never swerved from his duty to God or to men. And then he was banished, and driven away in disgrace, and fell at the feet of his spiritual fathers, crying out with great joy, 'Now I am stripped of all, and I begin to live indeed;' not I, but Christ in me.'

"Neither the dungeon nor the sanctuary was to shelter him long. He was to stand once more in the field of battle, with the green turf under his feet and the blue sky overhead. The Saxumans had invaded the kingdom of Bungo; their war-cry had been heard on the neighboring hills, their armies were gathered around Vosuqui, and Cicatondono stood alone in the city, without councillors and friends. The monarch and his sons were in a distant part of their dominions, and the brave old chieftain looked vainly around him for an arm as strong and a heart as dauntless as his own. Then he bethought him of the child of his adoption; of his banished, persecuted, Christian son; and the young hero was recalled to his side, and rode forth from the gates of the city amidst the warriors of Vosuqui. They were but a small band, and the Saxumans came to meet them with more than double their strength. Wild was the attack, desperate the encounter, fierce and long the conflict. The veteran soldier, Cicatondono, fought like a lion; but if he did prodigies of valor, who can describe the exploits of Cicatora, of the young Prince Simon? who can relate how he kept the enemy at bay, how he plunged into the thickest of the fight, calling on the God of the Christians, and commending himself to our Lady's protection? a hundred lances aimed at his breast, a hundred arrows flying around his head. But a cry from a distant part of the field has passed from mouth to mouth, and reaches his ears just as his victory seems secure. 'Cicatondono is sorely beset; Cicatondono has fallen!' Swift as the arrow from the bow the prince darts across the plain ; straight as the arrow from the bow his prayer speeds to the throne of God ; the Christian son has offered his life for that of his unbaptized father, and that prayer is the last his lips shall ever form. He falls upon the foe like the Archangel Michael on the rebel host. It is the soul of his father he is fighting for ; his arm is resistless ; he beats back the enemy, he clears the space around him, he shelters with his own the aged warrior's faint and bleeding form, and the soldiers of Vosuqui bear away from the field the wounded but living father, and the son, like a Christian hero, lies on the blood-stained field, with his sword in his hand and his crucifix on his breast."

When Anselm had ceased to speak, it was some little time before the silence which ensued was broken by the Queen. She had listened with breathless attention to his tale, and drew a deep sigh as he concluded it. Many and rich were the gifts she offered him when he left the palace that night, but one piece of money for himself, and one for the poor, was all he would accept, and it was but a small share of the first which went to his own support.

CHAPTER VIII.

A BAPTISM.

EARLY in the morning Grace hurried to the church a little before the usual hour of Mass. Anselm was standing near the door waiting for her. As she went up to him her heart was beating so fast that she could hardly speak. "Anselm," she said, "is the child who was born blind and miraculously cured at the college at Meaco, the same as the little boy they call Augustine?"

The old man nodded assent.

"Whose son is he?" she asked; in a trembling voice, and her heart sunk within her as he answered—

"I don't know, dear lady, I never asked."

"Then it is not the same child whom you saved from the river some six years ago, in the neighborhood of this place?"

He raised his hand to his forehead and reflected for a moment. In truth I cannot tell you—*that* child I took directly to some Christians in the neighborhood, who undertook the charge of it, and they may have sent him to the fathers at Meaco; but I know nothing about it."

"Can you tell me their names?" eagerly asked Grace.

"Yes; the husband was called James, and the wife Martha. I will go to them to-day and find out what they did with the child, as you seem anxious to know; and as her Majesty has commanded me to play again before her to-night, I will let you know the result."

After Grace had heard Mass, she asked to see Father Cespedes, and told him that the Queen's desire for baptism was becoming so irresistibly strong that she could no longer brook delay, and that she had formed a plan by which to accomplish her object. She had had a large case made in the shape of a coffin, and in the middle of the night she intended to be let down out of her window, and then by similar means over the outward walls of the palace, and then make her way to the church.

Grace explained this project with all the ardor of youthful impetuosity, and was greatly disappointed when the father charged her to dissuade the Queen from it. He pointed out to her that it was full of dangers of various sorts,—that if the plot was discovered, her Majesty's life might be endangered by the King's fury; and that she might be then exposed to die before she had received baptism; that she would risk not only her own safety, but that of her attendants, and be the cause, in all probability, of the suppression of the Church just reopened in Arima. "Tell the Queen to be patient," he added; "to watch, to fast, and to pray. Her wishes will soon be fulfilled, and you, my child, prepare yourself by many acts of devotion and humiliation for the performance of a duty which will soon perhaps be entrusted to you. Come to me again to-morrow; I have heard startling news to-day, but they need confirmation. We may all before long have to put on the armor of Christ, and brace ourselves for the conflict we are ever preparing for, since the day when our Lord said, 'The disciple is not greater than his Master; as they have persecuted Me, so will they persecute you.' God bless you, my child. Go amongst those new Christians in yonder palace, and be to them as the angel that walked by the side of the young Israelites in the fiery furnace. The Queen will need all the support your friendship can give her." Grace knelt down to receive the father's blessing, and hurried back to the palace.

She found the King in the Queen's apartments, and saw immediately that the latter was sorely disturbed. Fondasadono did not look angry, but he was talking loud and long of some news he had just heard. When grace entered the room he addressed himself to her. "Your father's friend, maiden, the sovereign to whom he is so devoted, has turned against the Christians; and people talk of an edict about to appear which will banish from the Ximo every priest of your religion. Justo will learn at last who are his friends and who his enemies."

"I think he has known that already," said Grace

calmly; "but duty and not feeling has been the rule of my father's conduct."

"The Kumbo-Sama has been in a fearful passion it is said. A Spanish sailor at Nangazaqui boasted the other day, as he sat in a house of public entertainment where some of the Emperor's officers happened to be present, that his Sovereign was the most powerful monarch in the world; and spreading out a map on the table he pointed to his possessions in every part of the world. 'How is it possible,' said one of the lords of the court, 'that your King can obtain possession of so many foreign countries?' 'Ah, that is easy enough,' the Spaniard answered; 'he sends the missionaries in the first instance to any kingdom he wishes to conquer; for some years they preach and make converts, and then, when the Christians are powerful enough, they drive out the reigning Sovereigns and bring in the King of Spain.'"

"Alas!" cried Grace, "what use the enemy of man makes of a fool! and what a dangerous thing it is to speak unadvisedly."

"Ah! but there is some truth in this statement," the King said, with a kind of sneering laugh; "you Christians are great disturbers of the peace of countries and families: you cannot deny that, maiden."

"In one sense I do; in another I do not," answered Grace earnestly; "we can promise you, if you become Christians, the deepest, the truest, the only real peace which can be known in this world."

"Ay; if we become Christians! but if we won't, you will not leave us in peace."

"No," said Grace again, in the same tone; "a Christian would not leave you in peace if he saw you unconsciously standing on the brink of a precipice, or asleep in the shade of the upas-tree, and he cannot leave you in peace whilst he hopes by any means to persuade you to renounce idolatry and receive the truth."

"You are young, and beautiful, and eloquent, Grace Ucondono; but you speak too confidently about your religion: there are no doubt some good points about it, but, after all, how can we tell what is truth?"

"That question was asked of Him who came on earth to found our religion; He did not answer it in words; He answered it by dying on a cross. There is not a Christian in Japan, Sire, who is not ready to give the Kumbo-Sama the same answer if he affords us the opportunity."

"I have sent to offer an asylum to your father and all your family in case they are included in this proscription; but no mention has been made of them in the report I have received. In the meantime I would recommend your priests to be prudent, and restrain their zeal within bounds. There is an amount of interference which no Sovereign can tolerate; and the authority of a husband, and that husband a king, is too absolute to brook the shadow of an opposition to his commands."

As Fondasadono uttered these words he cast a

severe glance on the Queen, whose color went and came as she leant on Grace for support. When he had left the apartment, her attendants gathered around her, and one and all declared that they were ready and eager to shed their blood for Christ's sake; and kneeling at her feet, passionately blessed her for having procured for them the inestimable blessing of the true faith. She wrung her hands and said, "Yes, you are happy: you have been baptized; what reck you of life or of death now that your sins have been washed away by the Sacrament of Baptism? You have no occasion to weep for yourselves, but you do well to weep for me. Oh, Grace, will not that father have to answer for my soul who refused to receive me into the Church, when kneeling at his feet I besought him with tears, and he would not hear me?"

Grace clasped her arms around her. She said, "Wait, and be patient for a few brief moments, beloved one; I will seek the father. But a few moments ago he spoke of you, and said you were soon to be baptized. Go into your oratory with all these Christian women; remain there in prayer before Mary's blessed image, and recommend yourself to her."

"Grace, I am frightened," said the Queen, turning very pale; "Fondasadono's eyes gleamed with fierce anger just now; you do not know him as I do; he leaves Arima to-day to go to Ozaca, but I fear what he may do on his return. If his passions are once roused he may persecute the Christians more fiercely than the Kumbo-Sama himself, and the more so that he once favored them. Oh! my heart sinks within me, and I have no strength for the conflict."

Grace bent over her, kissed her pale cheek and her cold hands, and then hurried to the house of the missionaries. When Father Cespedes saw her, he immediately said, "There is no time to lose, my child; the edict has gone forth at Meaco, and will probably extend to the tributary kingdoms. We cannot go to the Queen, and she cannot come to us. There is but one course left. Under the circumstances, it is not necessary that a priest should administer the sacrament of Baptism; to you, my child, it now belongs to fulfil the blessed duty. You have been long instructed in the mode of performing this act. Many a little infant, I have been told, has received spiritual life at your hands; is it so, my child?" Grace bowed her head in assent, for her heart was too full to allow her to speak. "Go then, and in the oratory where you assemble for prayer, gather together all the Christians in the palace, and in their presence baptize the Queen. It is a work of danger, Grace; it may involve you in a greater peril still than the one you have lately escaped. Are you afraid?"

"Afraid of my own unworthiness, father; of nothing else am I afraid."

"God bless you, my child. I will remain in

prayer before the Blessed Sacrament till you return or send me word that your holy task is accomplished."

When the Queen was told that Grace was to baptize her, by an irresistible impulse she prostrated herself before her. "At your hands, dearest; at your hands I am to receive this ardently desired blessing; then defer it not an instant."

Grace led the way to the oratory, and both knelt in fervent prayer; the Christian women standing around them with streaming eyes and joyful hearts. The life-giving water flowed on that careworn brow, and the words of grace and power were uttered slowly and distinctly in the hearing of all. Deep was the silence that followed. There are moments when the human voice dares not disturb the solemn intercourse that takes place between the soul and God, when prayer itself is voiceless, wordless in its intensity.

The Queen was the first to rise, and a great change visible to all had come over her. The strange light in her dark eyes was turned to a holy brightness. Faith was on her brow, hope in her smiles, and in the extended arms which she held out to all those young sisters in Christ who were crowding round her there was charity greater even than faith and hope.

"I am a Christian?" she exclaimed in a sacred transport; "now let the world do its worst; let the billows rage, let the winds roar, I am now within the ark."

Grace was gazing on her with surprise and awe: the change which baptism had wrought in her friend had been sudden and great; but in her own heart a more extraordinary one had taken place. She had ministered that sacred rite to another, and in the very hour when she had done so a new unearthly strain had rung in her ears, an echo of that song which those who follow the Lamb wheresoever He goes are eternally singing in the courts of heaven.

If that instant had been the beginning of a new spiritual life to "Mary" the Queen, for that blessed name had been given to her in baptism, it was to Grace that of a higher consecration, a more perfect self-abandonment. God had spoken to her soul: never again could earthly love gain a hearing from her, or earthly feelings share the affections of her heart. Not often is a change of this sort so sudden, so swift, so entire. Her vocation was revealed to her at once, and she was not disobedient to the heavenly vision. When death is hovering, as it were, in every breeze, and haunting us at every turn; when the world to come is a home close at hand, not a shadowy dream to be realized some far off day, the dealings of God with men's souls assume a more pressing character. There is then a reality in the spiritual life which gives no quarter, and rides roughshod over self-indulgent delays.

That same day Grace cut off her long hair; the sign with the Japanese women that they renounce the world and marriage. At the foot of the altar she made a vow for ever to lead a life of obedience, chastity, and poverty; to devote herself to the service of the poor, and join the first religious community of women that would come to Japan.

When she told Father Cespedes what she had done, he blamed at first the suddenness of her resolution, and the impetuosity with which she had acted. He even spoke with severity of the way in which she had disregarded an engagement sanctioned by her parents, and to which she had yielded her own full assent, but after she had opened her whole heart, and made known to him how direct and powerful had been the inspiration which had led her at once and for ever to consecrate herself to God, he suspended his judgment and feared to interfere with what he felt might be one of those exceptional ways in which he deals with privileged souls; especially in days of peculiar trial and fiery persecution. He charged her to confer with Father Organtin on her return to Meaco, and meanwhile to pray without ceasing for light and guidance.

As she came out of the church, Anselm met her at the door. "Lady," he said, "I have seen the people with whom the child was left. They took him with them the following year to Nangazaqui, and left him with the fathers; the boy that you saw at their college at Meaco is probably the same whom I saved from the river, and who was miraculously cured by the touch of Father Francis's handkerchief. Martha had taken from the child's neck this heathen charm; if you are making these inquiries with a view to finding out his parents, you had better take it with you. And now farewell, lady. I must travel quickly to Meaco. There are rumors of a persecution on foot, and that guards have been set at the house of the Spanish fathers, and of our own fathers also, and lists drawn up in which one might perhaps get one's name inserted. I am not going to miss such a chance."

"I too shall soon be returning to Meaco," said Grace; "the storm never rages but the lightning falls on our house, and death or exile are doubtless in store for us. Anselm, as you travel along say a great many Te Deums, for God's mercies to us have been great this day."

When she looked upon the charm which Anselm had left with her, Grace felt that she held in her hands what might at once clear up all doubts regarding the Queen's child, and she had a nervous fear of showing it to her, dreading the effect on her mind of the sight of this object, if she had indeed, as she supposed, placed it round the child's neck before he was taken from her. But events were hurrying on. She received a message that night from her father recalling her to Meaco, and alluding briefly to the menacing state of affairs as regarded the Christians. There was no time to lose; and after inducing the Queen to speak of the grief which had made such wild havoc in her heart, and which cast a shade even on her baptismal joy, she ventured to ask her if, before parting with her child, she had attached a charm to its neck.

The Queen looked at her with surprise. "Who has told you this, Grace? I know well it was a sin, but I did it in ignorance; our good God will forgive me. Why speak of it now? Oh, maiden, why probe a wound that never can be healed, not even by the blessing I have received this day, for my babe was unbaptized."

Grace unfolded the paper in which the piece of writing, encased in a small golden frame, was enclosed, and gave it into the Queen's hands, A wild expression came over her face. "Do you know it? Do you remember it?" Grace asked, hardly able to draw her breath.

"It is mine. It is the one; the very one. Oh, Grace, when, where, did you find it? Speak; I cannot bear the suspense."

"To-day Anselm gave it me—the musician."

"O my God! that child born blind he spoke of —that child at the fathers' house—that child cured by the relic! Oh, Grace, no, no, it cannot, cannot be. Oh Heaven! What is heaven! Earth is heaven if the child lives and is baptized!"

"He is baptized," said Grace in a voice of the deepest emotion; "he is a noble Christian child; on his fair brow and in his sweet eyes there is innocence; and royalty in his bearing."

Passionate were that mother's tears, passionate her thanksgivings; the rankling wound was healed, the aching void filled; the soul-consuming anguish for ever at an end. "Baptized," she kept repeating in a low voice, or else gazing at Grace in a kind of speechless ecstasy. She looked upon the charm which was lying on her knee. "It has touched his little neck," she said with an accent of inexpressible tenderness. But she deliberately rose, and was about to cast it into the brazier in the centre of the room.

"What are you doing?" said Grace, holding her hand.

"It is a thing accursed," she replied. "Can I to-day deny my God a sacrifice? Oh, Grace, I must die of gratitude at His feet."

"Yet stop; destroy it not; it may serve to identify the child."

"Do you think I wish to claim my boy? Oh, never; never in this world are these eyes to look upon him. Death, or a severe imprisonment, are about to be my portion. Grace, I know the King; perhaps he will not kill me, because my face is still pleasing in his eyes, and my conversation to his taste; but not one moment's freedom, not one moment's indulgence, have I to expect from him. If his sword does not pierce my heart, it will ever be pointed at my breast, and I shall live from day to day under sentence of death, for I shall tell him I am a Christian, and will continue so to my life's end; and do you think that if I could I would claim my son, and give him back to his heathen father? Do you think I would expose his soul to danger for the sake of resting my weary eyes upon his beloved face? of feeling his little hands round my

neck, and quenching in one moment the thirst of
the heart which for years has consumed me? Oh
no, not for all that this world could give of joy;
not to escape the long martyrdom which awaits me.
But you will see him, Grace; you will speak
to him of his mother; you will tell him how
her life is one long deep thought of him; how
his Christian mother will joyfully suffer any agony
that man can inflict if he but reaches the home in
the skies where one day she hopes to sit at his feet.
Oh yes, Grace, at his feet, for he must be far above
me there; my Christian boy, my baptized son,
reared in the shade of the sanctuary, at the feet of
Jesus, in the arms of Mary. Give him my blessing,
Grace; and oh, dearest of friends, and more than
friend, receive mine also. Thou hast been to me
far, far more than a mother or a sister. Thou hast
done well by me, Grace, and great will be thy reward; those bright locks cut off, those bright
earthly hopes renounced, that poverty embraced,
those are already pledges of what is reserved to
thee hereafter; the *best part;* the part that shall
never be taken away from those who have strength
to choose it. Wonder not to hear me speak thus
when on the very threshold of my Christian life; I
had been one so long in heart, I had prayed so
much for light, and in those hours of prayer many
things were revealed to me. And now farewell;
and may it be given to us both to die for the faith
of Christ, or to suffer much and long for His dear
sake.

CHAPTER IX.

PERSECUTION.

A GALLANT Spanish ship was breasting the waves, and making head against the rising storm, in the channel between China and Japan, the sea rolling heavily the while, and the sky above

"Dark as if the day of doom
Hung o'er Nature's shrinking head."

On board the heavily laden galleon were men of many nations as well as Spaniards, and amongst them a young man who wore the habit of St. Francis. This was Philip the Mexican, whose life had been spent, like the Prodigal's in the Gospel, far from his father's house, in vile riot and debauchery. In his native land he had incurred disgrace, and nearly broken his parent's hearts. In an hour of sorrow and repentance he sought admission amongst the Brothers Minor of the order of St. Francis; but his passions were too strong, and his will too weak, to persevere in the austerities of penance; he had thrown aside the cowl and plunged into the world again. Then in despair his father sent him to trade in China; and there the spendthrift came to himself. He saw what lives the missionaries led; he witnessed the fervor

of the native converts, and the miracles of grace
which religion works in the hearts of men, and his
soul recoiled at the sight of its own iniquities.—
Once more he entreated, this time most humbly, to
be clothed in the holy habit he had forsaken; and
he was now on his way home, where his parents,
overjoyed at the news of his conversion, had entreated that he might be sent back. Leaning
against the mast of the ship that night, he was
musing on the past, and a great fear seized him.
He remembered his former weakness, his broken
vows, his shattered resolutions. He gazed on the
billows, and the words of the patriarch to his first-
born son came into his mind: he felt that though
"excelling in gifts" he had indeed been "poured
out like water," and he clung to the mast of the
tempest-tossed bark as if it had been indeed the
raging sea that he was in fear of, and not that
wild ungovernable nature within him which had
so often proved more false and treacherous than the
ocean. He invoked the Penitent of Assisi and the
Apostle of the Indies, and commended himself to
her whose image was the figurehead of the struggling vessel, our Lady of Mount-Serrat. "Death,"
he murmured; "Death, rather than apostasy and
sin; death for Thee who died for me, my Lord."

The clouds at that moment opened, and on the
dark blue sky a white cross appeared, of the same
shape as those used in Japan for the execution of
criminals. Philip gazed upon it in silence. Did
others see it? He knew not, he cared not; to him

it seemed an answer to his prayer; a token that it
had been heard. It *had* been seen; it *had* been
hailed by some as a signal of hope, by others as an
evil omen. Every eye watched it; every heart on
board beat faster as the white cross became red, and
then, after a while, was enveloped in dark thick
clouds, and disappeared from sight.

Fiercer grew the tempest, and wilder the storm.
The ship drifted from its course at the mercy of the
wind and waves, and was driven at last into the
port of Urando, on the coast of Japan. This had
taken place some time before the events related in
the last chapter; and the capture of the vessel, in
connexion with other circumstances, had led to the
outburst of fury on the part of the Kumbo-Sama
which threatened the Christians with death and
banishment, and created a vehement excitement
from one end of the island to the other.

Philip had been sent from Urando to the convent
of his order at Meaco, and it was not long before the
cross he had seen in the skies assumed no longer a
visionary form. Burning with zeal, the sons of
St. Francis were defying the Emperor, and preaching the faith at Meaco as openly as they would
have done at Paris or at Rome. Strong in the
character they bore as envoys from the King of
Spain, they submitted to none of the restraints
which the Jesuit missionaries had accepted, and
rushed headlong into the breach, the cross in hand
and martyrdom in view. Then was exemplified
one of the peculiar characteristics of the Catholic

religion—variety in opinion, difference of spirits, combined with perfect unity of faith and sympathy of feeling. Those two holy bands, on the one hand the children of St. Francis, on the other the sons of St. Ignatius, were divided in council, and, like St. Peter and St. Paul in the days of old, withstood each other for a while on the line of conduct to be pursued in the midst of a heathen nation, and in the face of an infuriated despot. Not one of these apostolic men on either side but had long given away their lives to be held in readiness for the first summons to the gibbet or the cross; and to most of them death in any shape would have been the laborer's evening rest; the harvest-home of a long season of toil. But they differed as to the haste with which that goal was to be reached; they differed as to the course which would win most souls to Christ; they differed till it was time to die, then not a shadow of difference existed between them: hand in hand they walked to the scaffold, servants of *one* Lord, and apostles of *one* faith.

Meaco and all the principal towns in Japan were offering an extraordinary spectacle at that moment. Persons were hurrying to and fro with an appearance of eager and joyful excitement which had seldom been witnessed in that country, and which the European Christians of our day would find it difficult to understand. The houses of the missionaries were surrounded by guards; but it would have been natural to suppose that they were guards of honor, so great was the concourse of people, of all ranks, that were crowding their rooms and thronging their churches both night and day.— The Christian noblemen and officers of state surrounded the fathers, and openly declared that they were come to die with them, if such was to be their fate, or to follow them into banishment. The churches were filled with women: all the principal ladies of the town were assembled there, and the only thing that was clamored for on every side was that Father Baptiste, or Father Organtin, or Paul Michi, or Father Francis of St. Michael, should mount the pulpits of their respective churches and speak, as they knew how to speak, of the happiness of dying for Christ.

It was reported that lists were being made of all the Christians in Japan, and that all without exception were to be slain; and, with a few exceptions, the announcement (vibrating like an electric shock through the hearts of the baptised members of that heroic Church) had been received with a rapture which had never surely been known under similar circumstances since the days of St. Sebastian and St. Cecilia, of the Colosseum and the Catacombs.

Meanwhile, Guenifoin and Gibonoscio, the two principal magistrates of the town, were sitting with gloomy countenances inspecting the lists which had been made out by the Emperor's orders. They comprised their friends, their familiar acquaintances, their relatives even; and these two men felt their hearts sink within them as they saw in this sad muster-roll name after name of persons dear to them, which the edict, if confirmed and carried into execution, would involve in destruction.

"Heaven be praised," Guenifoin exclaimed (he made use in general of that expression, as not necessarily implying that he believed in the one only God of the Christians ; or, on the other hand, in the multifarious divinities of the Japanese religion). "Heaven be praised, Justo Ucondono is in great favor just now with the Kumbo-Sama, who will scarcely put to death one of his best generals before the peace with China is concluded ; and my son's beautiful affianced bride, his daughter, is at the Court of Arima, shut up in the palace with that poor Queen, whose face is not to be gazed upon by mortal eyes. Then Paul Sacondono is also two hundred leagues off, and deeply occupied with his governorship."

"But is he a Christian?" asked Gibonoscio.

"Oh, no, indeed," replied the Viceroy, with an uneasy look ; "I should never have suffered a son of mine to profess a religion different from the Emperor's. If these Christians would but be reasonable there is nothing really bad about them, or very shocking in their opinions ; but they are so intractable, so headstrong, so fanatical, I wish with all my heart they had never set foot in this country."

"Yet it is said that you always favor them."

"I never wished them to be persecuted, and they are very agreeable people to talk to, these fathers, so well informed, such able scholars; but Paul has seen too much of them. I was a fool to let him study Latin at their college."

The door opened at that moment, and Constantine, Guenifoin's youngest son, and his nephew, Michael, entered the room.

"What are you doing here?" exclaimed the Viceroy with alarm and displeasure, as the two young men presented themselves before him. "Why do you come to Meaco, my son, when I had ordered you to remain at Fuximi?"

"My father," said Constantine respectfully, "some days ago I met my cousin in the street, and he informed me of the proclamation against the fathers, and the edict which is prepared against the Christians. In the seclusion of Fuximi the news had not reached me. We went straight to the college and saw Father Organtin. My mind is made up, and so is Michael's, we are resolved to die with our spiritual fathers. We long for the day which will see us numbered with the martyrs; and we intend to do our utmost to merit this great mercy from our Lord. I have taken a lodging near the college, and there we will wait for the blessed hour which will open to us the gates of heaven."

Guenifoin had turned pale with grief and with anger. "Hush, foolish boy! You do not know what you are saying. You are not, and you never shall be, a Christian. All this silly talk is mere childishness."

"Father," said the young man earnestly, "you will not find it so. I have been baptized, and no earthly power can ever induce me to deny my faith. Before you, and before my lord," he added, bowing respectfully to Gibonoscio, "we are both come to declare ourselves Christians. We hear that you are drawing up these lists by the Emperor's commands; and our names must be enrolled in the number."

The unhappy father hid his face in his hands; his agitation was becoming uncontrollable; anger and affection were struggling in his breast. "It is news to me," he exclaimed, "that you have embraced the Christian religion, and sad news it is. Michael has seduced you," he added, looking sternly at his nephew; "the wily priests have ensnared you both. How dare you, young as you are, fly in the face of your Sovereign and your parents? Beware what you do. If the Emperor commands me to put all the Christians to death, you must not expect to find mercy. There are precedents enough, in ancient and modern times, of parents killing their own children for rebelling against their princes."

The two young men knelt at the feet of the Viceroy, and Constantine, embracing his knees, replied in these words: "Father, it is not the fear of death that moves me to this confession, but anxiety for your interest, lest some misfortune should come upon you in consequence of my resolution. You tell me we are obliged to obey the

King; how much more the King of kings, the Lord of heaven and earth, who first gave and still preserves this being of ours? I am ready, my father, to die by your hands, or in any other way, as it shall please God to appoint; if you put me to death, you only take away the life you gave, and bestow upon me a better one in its stead; but if others take this duty upon them, I shall have the consolation that you will be innocent of my blood, and not exposed to the self-reproach you might one day feel at having killed your own child. God is my witness: I am ready to obey you in everything where my soul's interest is not in question: but you, who have always shown me so great and tender an affection, cannot require of me that, in order to please a prince, I should forfeit the happiness of heaven."

"Talk not to me of happiness, or of heaven! we are dealing with realities now, not with the dreams of a visionary future. I loathe the very sound of those high-sounding words; molest not my ears with them; but comply with my orders at once. You shall join your brother at Tamba, and carry letters to him from the Governor."

Constantine hesitated an instant; he felt deeply for his father, for the poor old man's hands were trembling, and tears were forcing their way down his cheeks, in spite of his efforts to conceal them. Once more he knelt and clasped his knees—"Dear, dear, father, the truth must be told. Paul Sacondono is at this moment at Meaco; at the college, preparing by a general confession of his whole life for the happiness of martyrdom."

"Then accursed be the day in which these seducers set their foot in this land—accursed be the hour when they set eyes on my children—the gods—"

"Oh, father, father, speak not so wildly, so falsely; call not upon gods in whom you believe not, and do not curse Father Francis. You have often told me that you had seen him when you stood at your mother's knee; and that if ever a man bore the stamp of a messenger from God it was he. And you have loved Father Organtin—"

"And I should love him still, and be myself a Christian, perhaps, if Christians had a grain of sense, or of prudence. If it were not for that headstrong, intolerant obstinacy, which destroys the peace of families and brings ruin upon our houses. Oh, Constantine, my son, my beloved child, disguise this faith of yours for a while, as you would not have your aged father die of grief."

"Disguise!" said the youth, bursting into tears. "No, my father, I cannot disguise the truth. I cannot deny my faith."

"Then I will cut your throat with my own hands," cried Guenifoin, exasperated. But the words had scarce passed his lips, when sorrow again prevailed, and he said, "To attempt my son's life would be my own death."

Paul Sacondono had hurried to the capital at the first intelligence of the imperial edict against the fathers. He was a young man of great promise; of wonderful abilities. His studies had been deep, and his passion for knowledge in the first instance attracted him to the missionaries. The threatened persecution roused all the latent ardor of his character. His whole soul, like that of so many of his countrymen, was bent on martyrdom; and he made the sacrifice of his life with a fervor which seemed to change the whole current of his thoughts and feelings. Paul Michi, his countryman, was also his intimate friend; to him he opened his heart. He had made that day a review of his whole life, and he had weighed both the past and the future in the light of the sanctuary. He saw the past, full of sins, forgiven indeed, but unexpiated; the future, short, uncertain, perilous.

"Paul," he said, as his friend and himself paced to and fro in the alleys of the college garden, "if religion was firmly established in this land of ours; if we had churches, not daily and hourly threatened with destruction; if we had schools for our children, and native priests ordained in sufficient number, then indeed would it be time for Christians to think of marrying; but it seems to me, that at present, if we indulge in such projects, we are like those persons before the Flood, who sat down to eat, to drink, and to play; who married and were given in marriage, even whilst the awful waters were gathering from the deep to swallow them up. My soul sickens at the thought. There is other work for a man to do than to sit at home at ease. It is no time for dreams of love and for domestic enjoyments when God's servants are about to die, and the blood of our brethren, if not our own, is soon to flow. Even now, when I was in the church offering my life to God if He pleased to take it, I felt as if a voice was saying to me, 'Thy life is accepted, whether thy blood is required or not.' I cannot shake off this impression. I have seen at Ozaca those noble youths (the four ambassadors, who went to Europe only to learn to despise the world by a trial of its pomps, its joys, and its pleasures), I have seen them there humble novices, patient learners in the school of perfection; and that internal voice whispered to me again, 'Go and do thou likewise.' My spirit assents to the call and longs to dedicate this wretched body to the service of God; to the cross, if it may be so, or to the daily dying to self which it witnesses here. But I am engaged to be married (you know it, my friend) to Justo Ucondono's virtuous daughter. Can I break that engagement formed by our parents and ratified by mutual consent? Advise me."

Paul Michi was a man of great spiritual discernment; of much knowledge and eloquence. On this occasion, however, he did not waste many words on Paul Sacondono. His advice was comprised in one single syllable—"Wait;" and the best proof of a religious vocation in the latter was the submission with which he accepted that answer, subdued the keen longings for action which were agitating his soul, and acquiesced in suspense, the keenest of trials to an ardent spirit.

CHAPTER X.

PREPARATION.

In Agatha's house a number of pious women had assembled for the purpose of preparing garments for the time of their execution; for the general impression was, that the list of Christians, which it was well known had been made, was drawn up for the purpose of putting all to death who did not renounce their faith. Nothing could exceed the calm joyfulness with which they set about this task. They sung pious hymns, and related, each in turn, the stories which they had heard or read of the martyrs in other lands. As they spoke of Cecilia —and the angel who crowned her with flowers, and was only visible to her husband's eyes when he had been baptized, and renounced forever the right of looking upon her as his wife—their eyes involuntarily turned upon Grace Ucondono, who had taken her place amongst them as usual. Her dress was changed; the expression of her countenance was altered; there was in her face a deeper peace, a more heavenly sweetness. A heavy weight had that morning been removed from her heart. Immediately after her return, she had disclosed to her father the strange and sudden change which had taken place in her feelings after she had administered the sacrament of Baptism to the Queen of Arima, and entreated him to announce it to Paul Sacondono. He bade her in the first instance seek Father Organtin, and take his advice. That holy man had been praying long and earnestly both for her and for Paul, and when his eyes fell on her altered dress, and the first words she addressed to him were these—"Father, I can never marry: I have given my heart to God, and no earthly love can ever find place in it again," he remained silent a moment, and then the only words he uttered were, "Thank God."

They were not made for this world's common happiness, these two ardent spirits; these two well-matched souls, whose sympathy had been deeper than they knew or could have foreseen, their characters were formed in no ordinary mould, and the times and the country in which their young lives had been cast were fitted for the heroic exercise of more than common virtue. They met for an instant: they blessed each other fervently, and prayed before the altar, where they had once thought to stand as bridegroom and bride. It was no time for that; they felt it to their very hearts' core. They formed a still holier union as they knelt there that day. Never would the one forget the other in prayer; never would they cease to plead for each other, before the tabernacle, at the altar, or on the cross. The promise was made; the pledge was given; then each rose in silence.

They looked not back. They spoke not again.
He crossed the threshold of the noviciate ; and she
went to Agatha's house, and worked at the dresses
which were even then being got ready for the day
of martyrdom. No wonder that she looked like
St. Cecilia ; no wonder that her beauty had grown
more ethereal, and that she walked this earth as
one who had but little to do with its hopes or its
cares.

Agatha was thoughtful. She begged the prayers
of her companions for an intention she had much
at heart, and though nothing could ruffle her temper it was evident that she was suffering from
anxiety. She knew that her husband Andrew
was at that very moment gone to announce to his
aged father the proclamation of the edict against
the Christians, and she felt uneasy as to the effect
this might have on the mind of the old warrior,
who had but recently been received into the
Church.

This Mark Ongasamara was a fine specimen of a
Japanese soldier. Though he was fourscore years
of age his energy was unabated, and the vigour of
his soul far outstripped the weakness of his body.
He had embraced Christianity from deliberate conviction, after many conversations with the missionaries ; but he retained a great attachment for the
traditions and the customs of his country. He had
been heard to argue with the fathers, that for a
man to die by his own hands when a point of
honour required it could not be offensive to God or

inconsistent with Christianity. And though he had been obliged to give in, there was always a struggle going on in his mind between the obligations of his new faith and the all but unconquerable prejudices of his country and his ancient mode of thought.

His son approached the subject in the plain, uncompromising manner which characterized his countrymen on all matters of religion: "My father," he said, when the venerable old man had simply nodded his head in assent to the announcement that all Christians in the Empire were about to be doomed to death. "My father, as you have been so lately baptized, perhaps you do not quite understand the nature of martyrdom. The greatest favour that God can bestow on a Christian is to offer him an occasion of laying down his life for His sake. But whoever aspires to this crown must be very meek and humble, and ready to receive without opposition, and on his knees the fatal blow."

The old man started up as if he had been shot, and drawing his sword, exclaimed: "What! a man of honour as I am to let himself be murdered like a coward, and not dispute his life? To see the heathens butcher before our eyes those fathers that made us Christians, and quietly look on Andrew? you cannot mean that. Let me see whether the wretches will dare to lay hands upon them. I'll hew down seven or eight of them at my feet, and then, if they kill me fighting in this manner, I

*15

am willing to die a martyr, but not in any other way."

Andrew made another attempt. "You know, my father," he said, "that the family of Ongasamara has been always famous in Japan for its valour and noble exploits. As for yourself, you have given the world so many instances of your courage, that none would dare to bid you defiance who were not weary of life, so that it cannot be ascribed to cowardice if you should quietly submit to death. But if you cannot make up your mind to it, my dear father, why not retire into the country, with my little son, till the persecution has passed away? In this manner you will preserve the name of our family and the glory of our blood."

The old man firmly clenched his sword, and hastily cried out, "Retire yourself, if you like; I'll stand my ground. It shall never be said that Mark Ongasamara refused to look an enemy in the face. No, no, my son, neither of your proposals suit your old father. I'll break some of their heads, and then die a martyr."

Andrew sighed and withdrew, with no hope but in the prayers which he knew were being put up for the brave but obstinate old man.

Later in the day, Mark was wandering about the house, grumbling against his son, abusing the Emperor, calling the heathens scoundrels, and the Christians fools, when he happened to open the door of the room where his daughter-in-law with her children and her friends were sitting at work.

He stood a moment looking on their calm and happy faces; their fingers were busily occupied making up various dresses, and the little children were sitting at their feet, stringing beads for rosaries or making cases for relics. His eyes rested on Grace's countenance, which was beaming with more than ordinary joy, and the sweet smile with which she greeted him, so full of sweetness, peace, and hope, went straight to the old man's heart. The scene before him was an extraordinary one—there was animation, cheerfulness, a sort of gaiety even in its aspect, but he could not but feel that all this joy was of a peculiar nature. He felt puzzled. There was a large crucifix on the table, and he saw that the eyes of the workers, and even of the young children, were frequently turned towards it with a look of intense affection and reverence. "What are you so busy about?" he said, advancing into the room, and taking hold of the garment which his daughter-in-law held in her hand. She looked up unto his face, and her own flushed with a feeling deeper than words could express, as she answered:—

"We are preparing our festal robes for the day when we are to die for Him"—she bowed her head and pointed to the crucifix.

"And these young girls, and these children?" Mark inquired with a faltering voice.

The youthful voices rose with one accord—"We are all going to die for Jesus."

He caught in his arms one little fellow who could

hardly speak plain, and who held a rosary in his hand—"What shall you say, child, when they ask you if you are a Christian?"

"I'll confess the truth."

"But if they seek to take away your life, and prepare to crucify you, what will you do then?"

"I'll prepare for death."

"In what manner?" added the old man.

The child disengaged himself from his grandfather's embraces, stretched out his little arms, and replied again—"I'll cry out as long as I can speak, Mercy, Jesus; Mercy, Jesus; Jesus have mercy on me."

The aged warrior heaved a deep sigh from the depths of his full heart. "God bless thee, child; thou wilt never be a coward or an apostate; the spirit of the Ongasamaras lives in thee, my boy. But wilt thou not fight the men who would slay the fathers?"

The boy thought for a moment; and then said, "If I am to be a martyr I must not fight. Father Baptiste told me so."

Mark remained silent for a second; grace and pride were struggling in his heart; the conflict was sharp, but the victory at last complete. He drew his poniard from his side, unsheathed it, gazed for an instant on the shining blade, then dashed it on the ground. "Give me that crucifix," he cried, and seizing the image of his dying Lord, he clasped it to his breast. "This shall be my only weapon. I too will die a martyr. Where is Andrew?"

His son went with him to the college, where Father Organtin was just arrived, and Father Rodriguez had joined him. The house was thronged with Christians, many of them trying to persuade the Rector to retire, while there was yet time, to Nangazaqui, but the Father's mind was made up, and it was in vain that his flock urged his departure.

"Let others do as they please," he said; "for my own part I know what becomes my age and profession; I have laboured for these twenty years and upwards to establish the Christian religion in this place, and now that we have to combat in its defence would you have me fly and hide myself? God forbid that I should abandon my poor children. I know what is my duty to God, and to the Society to which I have the happiness to belong. In Meaco I remain, come what may. I'll seal with my blood the truths I have preached, and animate the Christians, by my example, to die for Jesus Christ."

Guards had not yet been set on the college; some of the heathens who were friendly to the missionaries called to give them information of the state of affairs. Some of the bonzes had been calling on Guenifoin and Gibonoscio to proceed to the execution of the threats against the Christians, and insisted upon it that the lists which had been drawn up, and which some of their agents had been actively collecting, were intended by the Emperor to decide the fate of all those whose names were enrolled in them. Justo Ucondono's and Guenifoin's two sons were included in the number, as well as the Jesuit and Franciscan fathers, and all those who were supposed to frequent their churches. Guenifoin, dismayed and miserable, did not venture to oppose the bonzes. Human respect was struggling in his heart with natural affection; but Gibonoscio indignantly refused to submit to the dictation of these men.

"You do not seem," he said, "rightly to understand the Emperor's pleasure. It is not his design to put all the Christians to death—that would be a horrible slaughter—his aim is only to destroy the more notorious offenders, and such as openly bid defiance to his laws. I perceive that you have got Justo Ucondono's name at the head of your list. Is it any news to any of us that Justo is a Christian? Has he not been often in danger of his life for the same reason, and thrice gone into banishment? The Emperor has since recalled him, and he is, whether you know it or not, in great favour with him. How are we to distinguish who are Christians and who are not? How can you tell that I am not one? How can I tell that you are not? As to the house of the Jesuits, I have not thought it proper to set guard on the residence of his Majesty's interpreter. I know my own business, and what belongs to my office, and I have no doubt of being able to satisfy the Emperor as to my conduct."

Justo Ucondono had gone early that day to take

leave of the King of Conga, who had showered favors upon him at the time of his last banishment. He was at Fuximi, and there Justo, with the warmest expressions of gratitude, gave him as a remembrance two valuable vases of very great price, and told him that he had wished to see him once more before his death, which was near at hand.

Chicagundono tenderly embraced him, but protested that he was at the Court at the time that the sentence was passed, and that he was certain that it only concerned the Spanish religious. "I heard the Emperor say in the most positive manner that it was not his intention to include in it the Jesuit fathers and their followers; therefore, my beloved friend, take courage, the sentence does not touch you."

"Sire," answered the Christian hero, "you say this to console me; and may the only true God, whom I have served from my youth up, reward you for your charity; but you do not know what the feelings of Christians are when they have once conceived the hope that they may be admitted to die for their religion. It is a joy to which no other joy can be likened; and the news has spread through our community like the sound of the trumpet calling warriors to battle. You know, sire, how that sound thrills through the heart and animates the soul, and yet that feeling is tame when compared to the rapture a Christian feels when he hears the word 'Martyrdom.' "

"Justo," exclaimed the heathen king, throwing

his arms around him, "thy religion is a strange one, but if it has made thee what thou art I cannot hate it. Is it true that thy daughter, the lily of the Ximo, the jewel of great price, has cut off her radiant locks, and abjured marriage and the world?"

"It is true," answered Justo; "one of those singular inspirations of divine grace which man cannot suggest, but to which he must submit, impelled her to this course. And the youth to whom she was betrothed, Guenifoin's eldest son, at the same time, almost at the same moment, conceived the desire of a life of higher perfection and more complete dedication to God's service than that which both of them had for a while anticipated; and, in troth, for Christians in this country and this time it is idle to dwell on thoughts of earthly happiness. We have no resting-place for our feet, no shelter for our heads. Our home is not here. Why should we build ourselves huts in the wilderness on our way? The glorious heaven will soon be reached by a short, and, it may be, by a bloody road."

The friends parted, and Justo returned to Meaco. Business had summoned away to Ozaca Father Organtin. The missionaries there were equally threatened with those of Meaco, and wished to confer with the Provincial on matters connected with the obligations of Christians in these perilous times. Three Jesuits, two fathers and one lay brother, remained at the College, and with them the little boy in whom Grace was so deeply interested. At her return from Arima she had been to see the child, and no sooner had she beheld him than his likeness to his mother was apparent to her. No doubt remained in her mind as to his identity with the royal babe doomed to death, but wonderfully rescued from a watery grave. Those deep set and somewhat mournful looking eyes, the sweet expression of the mouth, and a certain gracefulness and dignity of carriage, in this young boy reminded her irresistibly of the heroic and persecuted Christian Queen. She entered into conversation with Augustine; she asked him what he most desired; what she could give him which would please him.

The child smiled, and said, "Is it the lady I dreamed of that has told you to ask?"

Grace started. "What lady do you mean, Augustine?"

"I had heard it read in the refectory one day, that our Lord had appeared to St. Catherine, and showed her two crowns, one of roses, and one of thorns like His own, and asked her which she would have, and that she chose the latter. It was a hot day in the summer, and when the fathers went into the church I fell asleep in the garden, in the shade of that tall camelia-tree which you see there, near the window; and I dreamt that I saw a lady who held in one hand a crown of beautiful flowers, and in the other a cross. She asked me which I would have; and I said the crown of flowers. Then her face seemed to me to turn very white, and she looked like the marble statue of the Blessed Virgin. She shook the wreath, and many serpents fell out from amongst its leaves. Then I cried out, 'I'll have the cross,' and when she gave it me, red and white roses had grown out of it, and when I opened my eyes I found that a branch of the camelia-tree had fallen on my knees. Brother Paul does not like me to talk of my dreams; he says they mean nothing; but I think I shall one day see that lady again; and when I hear everybody talking, as they do now, about Christians being crucified, I always think that in that dream I chose the cross, and that the red and white flowers meant something."

"Innocence and martyrdom, perhaps," murmured Grace; "O happy little child, if God has marked thee out to bear company to the slaughtered babes of Bethlehem. Tell me, Augustine, wouldst thou not like to be a prince, and live like the Kumbo-Sama, in a great palace, and ride at the head of a great number of troops?"

"Yes; I should like to be a prince in the kingdom of Heaven, and live in God's great palace in the skies; and I should like to ride at the head of the white-robed army of martyrs, and follow the Lamb whithersoever He goes."

"My boy," said Grace, kneeling down, and throwing her arms round the child, "there is a lady who thinks of you, and prays for you."

"My mother Mary, in heaven?"

"I dare not call the one I speak of your mother,

sweet boy ; she has made you over to one whom you truly name your mother. But on earth also there is a woman that loves you, Augustine."

"Has she a crown and a cross in her hands?"

Grace felt the strange truth of the interpretation of the child's dream. "Perhaps she has. Which shall she send you?"

"The cross," said the boy unhesitatingly. "The cross means, to die for the love of Jesus ; and that is what I mean to do, if that cruel brother Paul Michi does not shut me up when they all go to be crucified. Do you know, lady, that some time ago I went to the Porziuncula Convent with Brother Paul, and Brother Gotto, and Brother Kisai, to walk in the procession, and scatter flowers before the Blessed Sacrament; and aftewards I was playing with Lewis and Anthony, when the Bonze Faxegava came to write down the names of all the Christians who were there. They wanted to leave out Lewis, and Anthony, and me, but we cried so dreadfully, and begged so hard, that at last Faxegava looked at us with great anger, and put down our names ; though the Father Commissary tried to get us out of the way. Then they made us all stand in a row, and counted how many we were: there were twenty-four names, and for some time only twenty-three of us in a row ; but then the lay brother, Matthias, came in, and that made twenty-four. He must be very ill, poor Matthias : he looked so dreadfully white, I thought he was going to fall down. And now, lady, the bell is ringing, and I must go. Ask the lady you spoke of to send me or bring me a cross; and come and see me again."

Grace kissed the child, and when she went home wrote to the captive Queen of Arima what was the gift that her infant son desired at her hands.

CHAPTER XI.

MISGIVINGS.

DAYS went by, days of alarm and prayer, of fervor and suspense. The Emperor was at Fuximi pressing on some fresh preparations for the ceremonies which the earthquake and his subsequent retirement had interrupted. The enemies of the Christians were besetting him on all sides, and urging the execution of the edicts against them. Faxegava, on the one hand, was bent on their destruction, and Gibonoscio, on the other, striving by every means in his power to avert the threatened slaughter. Meantime, the Christians all over the country—the priests and the people, the royal converts in palaces which had become to them prisons, the poor in their humble abodes, little children in the midst of their sport—were preparing their souls for death, and encouraging each other against the day of martyrdom.

The causes of the persecution were nearly lost sight of. The unhappy man who by his rash and ill-advised words placed in jeopardy the whole Church of Japan has sailed away from its shores, unconscious, perhaps, of the harm he had done; leaving behind him a memorable instance, well fitted "to point a moral and adorn a tale," of the mischief wrought by that little member which St. James calls "the unquiet evil." In the mean time, the holy missionaries devoted themselves to their spiritual children with unwearied assiduity. Restraining the most impetuous of their neophytes from rushing needlessly into danger, encouraging the timid, and instructing all to meet with meekness as well as courage their approaching fate. Father Organtin writes to his superior at Goa—"Great news, reverend father; great news to all our hearts' content. We have advice that the Emperor has given positive orders to put to death all the religious at Meaco and Ozaca. Brother Paul is so transported with it that he can hardly contain himself. 'Now, brethren,' he goes about saying, 'our vows are accomplished, and we shall die for the love of Him who first died for us.' The news filled us all with extreme joy, and we instantly began to prepare for martyrdom. What adds to our comfort, and strengthens us in these resolutions, is the admirable example of Christians of all sorts, who are ready to sacrifice all and lay down their lives for the faith of Jesus Christ. Justo Ucondono particularly distinguishes himself on this occasion, and so do the two sons of Guenifoin, the Governor of Meaco. They never leave us in all these troubles. It would be tedious to number up all the other Christians who aspire to martyrdom. God grant that we may die so as to deserve eternal life in heaven." And from the Franciscan Convent of the Porziuncula, the Japanese Santa Maria degli Angeli, the heroic and saintly Father Peter Baptiste, addresses his brethren in a similar strain:—

"We have been two days close besieged by a troop of soldiers. All the Christians are condemned to die. The first day that our house was invested the Christians confessed, and spent the whole night in prayer. Father Francis and I, upon information from some of the principal Christians that we were to die next morning, spent the whole time in hearing confessions. I communicated all our brethren and fifty Christians in form of Viaticum; after that, every one provided himself with a cross to carry in his hand at the time of execution. The Christians here express such an ardent desire of martyrdom that they rob me of my heart. The neighbors assist us more liberally than ever with their charitable alms. How things will end is yet uncertain; some think that we shall be sent back to Europe, and others that we shall die. Assist us with your holy prayers, that we may deserve this mercy from His Divine Majesty."

There was joy and peace in many a threatened home, and as men walked about the streets they could almost have told who were Christians by the bright look which their faces wore. In the college and in the convent there was a joyful exultation, which found vent in hymns of praise and fervent thanksgivings at the foot of the altar.

But in the house where Laurentia was sitting (as on the day when this little story began) there was an anxious, sorrowful heart. Oh, it is easy to bear a straightforward trial, however sharp, however heavy; but as "hope deferred makes the heart sick," suspense, and fear, and misgiving wear it out.

Laurentia had never returned to the royal household since the disasters of Fuximi. The timid Empress had stifled her inclination towards the Christian religion, and cancelled the appointments she had made before the Christians had incurred the Kumbo-Sama's displeasure. Truth had flashed before her eyes like the lightning, which we gaze at as something beautiful, but which we dare not fix our eyes upon lest it should blind us by too much brightness. The mind was feeble, the will powerless; she had groped in the darkness, and sighed for light; but when the earth shook, and the sky flashed with lurid fires, she had shrunk back affrighted, and given up the search, and now she almost hated, (if so weak a character could be said to hate anything) the very name of that creed which taught men to suffer and to die. She sent for the most eloquent of the bonzes to discourse to her in flowing periods, and disprove the distasteful truths of the foreign religion ; and then, soothed and satisfied, she glided over the stream of life, shuddering at each ripple on its surface, and never looking into the depths beneath.

This had been a sorrow to the Christian maiden, but there was, for a while, in her soul such a well-spring of happiness that it seemed to flow forth and cover with its bright waves every sad spot in her thoughts or in her life. Isafai's love was the spell which threw light on every present hour, every future prospect. He was so good, so noble, so generous, so tenderly true to her, his bride, his affianced wife. She rested upon his love not as an obstacle, but as a support on her way to heaven. When the threatened persecution was announced, she felt a strange thrill in her heart. We can but die together, she thought; and even martyrdom seemed to her more glorious and more precious if shared with him. A few sighs escaped from her as she thought of that little home they were to have dwelt in by the blue waters of the Corean sea, of the plans they had formed, of the hopes they had indulged, of the bright visions of the few last months swallowed up in a grander and a deeper vision, which enfolded them both in its glorious rays, but in which she feared to lose sight of him whom she felt so far in advance of her in the road to heaven. But after she had seen him and spoken with him, the spirit which animated him became hers. She had then no fears, no misgivings for him or for herself, but still her heart was not at ease; she trembled at every fresh report of the approaching persecution; she listened with dread to the sound of every footstep. To no one, not even to Isafai, did she confide her fears, only to Father Rodriguez her confessor. But her grief was one which even he had not much power to allay. She took every pretext of going to the

Franciscan Convent; but she seldom could see her brother. He avoided her. Once she met him on his way to a neighboring village, where he was going to instruct a catechuman, and they exchanged a few words, standing under a palm-tree by the wayside.

He spoke of her approaching marriage, and told her that he was going to make over to her all his property. He was soon to become a religious, and hoped never to leave the holy order of St. Francis. "Sister," he said to her earnestly, "whatever happens, never cease to pray for me."

"Whether you live, or whether you die, dearest brother," she said, "I can never cease to do so."

"Ay, but there may be a state worse than death, and not to be called life; pray for me even then."

She looked at him with some alarm; she fancied he might be speaking of insanity.

He read her thoughts, and said, "No, sister, there is nothing wild in my words or in my mind; it is not that I am afraid of; but I have not faith enough—I cannot trust myself."

"But cannot you trust God, Matthias?"

"I try," he said, clasping his hands nervously; "but those children at the convent, they torture me; they are always, ignorantly, poor infants, putting before me in a tangible form what I dare not allow myself to think of, unless sometimes on my knees before the altar or the crucifix, and then I feel such a wretched hypocrite. I am now about to instruct others in truths which I believe in indeed, but—"

"O brother, which you would die for!"

"Laurentia, if ever—if ever you should hear your brother has apostatized, do not curse him, but pray for him." And so they parted that day in silence and in grief.

Gibonoscio had pleaded long and earnestly the cause of the Christians with the Kumbo-Sama, and many of the heathen princes, at the request of Austin the High Admiral, of Simon Condera, Justo Ucondono, and other Christian nobles, came forward to support his efforts in behalf of the Christians in general, and in particular of the Jesuit fathers. One day when they were in company with him at Fuximi, whilst he was visiting the new buildings which he was erecting on the spot where his former palaces had been laid low, they ventured to represent to him that these fathers, during the forty years they had spent in Japan, had never been known to intrigue against the state or to meddle with any business that might give disturbance to the public. "Sire," said one of these courtiers, "although I am no Christian I have often heard these men preach. They teach men to obey their superiors, to be reconciled to their enemies, to comfort the afflicted, to relieve the poor, to visit the sick, and assist them to the utmost of their power. In a word, they appear to extend good to all and hurt to none."

As the Emperor listened patiently, and with some tokens of approbation to this speech, Guenifoin took courage, and said, "Sire, these fathers have always showed respect and deference to your Majesty's orders in all the Ximo, as well as at Meaco; and Father Organtin, even though he has the imperial permission for residing there, lives in great retirement, like a banished person, has changed his habit, and never appears in public."

The Emperor stood for a moment in deep thought, and then said: "There are four reasons which would induce me, at least for the present, to spare the lives of the Jesuit fathers,—First, if I were to slay all their priests at once, it might infuriate the Christians of the Ximo, and stir them up to revolt; then, I do not wish to quarrel with the Portuguese traders; then also, the new Christian Bishop has brought me some fine presents from the Viceroy of the Indies; and then, those fathers themselves have been wise and prudent in their conduct."

A breathless silence followed that speech. The Emperor turned away and said no more at that time, and Guenifoin went in search of Gibonoscio to whose hands the execution of the edict had been committed.

Gibonoscio, in consequence, hurried that evening to the palace. "Sire," he said, kneeling at the Kumbo-Sama's feet, "your Majesty commanded me yesterday to put to death the Christian fathers. Are those that came in the Portuguese vessels included in the number?"

"No," replied the Emperor; "I condemned none but those that arrived in the Philippian galleon.

They are traitors, who reduced Mexico to the obedience of Spain, and are come here to play the same tricks, but they shall not impose on Taico Sama. If their law was good I should give leave to my interpreter, Father Rodriguez, and his brethren, to teach it: for they have always a regard to my commands, but those newcomers have openly defied me. Let them be put to death, and all who were in the house the day that the edict was proclaimed, and never heard of again. But go to my interpreter, and tell him from me to keep a good heart, and see that no injury is offered to the Bishop at Nangazaqui."

Late that evening there was a strange mixture of joy and sorrow, of lamenting and rejoicing, in Meaco. The Christians heard that the guards were taken off the Jesuits' College, and they crowded round their fathers and masters in the faith and wept tears of joy at their release. But the noble band in the Franciscan Convent, the fathers of that order, their lay brothers, their catechists, the two young boys under their care, the three Jesuit brothers, and the little child who had been with them on the day when the fatal list was drawn up, were irrevocably doomed to death. The Emperor's will had been declared. The subject was never to be again broached in his presence. The death-warrant of the twenty-four victims included in that list had gone forth, and that number must die!

It would have been hard to tell that day which

were the victims, which the reprieved. Tears fell from the eyes of Father Organtin, and many of his companions and spiritual children wept aloud. "My son," said the superior, "God has crowned the zeal of those holy men, the Franciscan fathers, and reserves us for harder conflicts. But the child Augustine, cannot he be saved?"

Augustine was sought for in the College, but was nowhere to be found. He had overheard the news, and had fled to the Franciscan Convent; there he hid himself behind a pillar in the church, and when he heard that the officers of the Emperor were come to make sure of the appearance of all the condemned persons, he came forward, and cried with a loud voice, "I am Augustine; my name is on the list."

Father Baptiste pleaded for the child, and besought the Bonze Faxegava to spare his life, and send him back to the College of the Jesuits. The heathen priest would not consent to that last proposal, but offered to take the boy with him to the Temple of Amida, and educate him in the Japanese religion.

Augustine hearing these words, cried out, "Father Peter, I will not live without you. Do not send me to the temple where they worship devils. Take me to heaven with you, father. God will not be pleased with you if you leave me with His enemies."

Anthony and Lewis, who were a little older than Augustine, came forward also, and both clung to the superior's knees, and besought him to let them die for Christ.

The aged Christian looked steadily at the children, and then raised his eyes in silent prayer to heaven. He dared not bid them depart; he dared not consign them to the idolatrous impostor. He laid his shrivelled hand on their young heads, and said "So be it then, my children. We will not part company in this world; and if it please Him to have mercy on me, not in the next world either."

The bonze turned pale with rage, for he had no power to remove the children whose names were in the fatal but blessed list of martyrs. He threatened them with dreadful torments, but their courage was invincible, and their firmness not to be shaken.

Meanwhile, all the prisoners have assembled in the hall, and the muster-roll was called; one of them was missing; his non-appearance was accounted for: he had been sent on a distant errand by the orders of the Father Commissary, but was shortly to return.

"You will answer then for his appearance tomorrow," cried Faxegava; "not with your own lives, which are already forfeited, but by those of every priest and Christian in Meaco, for mark my words if every one of the criminals in this list is not brought up for execution on the appointed day, the Emperor's clemency will be withdrawn, and vengeance overtake the whole rebellious set of foreign intruders, who overrun Japan with their pestilent doctrines. If this Matthias is not forthcoming by to-morrow at noon I shall denounce all your secret admirers, your cunning abettors, the traitor Guenifoin and the cowardly Gibonoscio. If your detested names are breathed again in the Kumbo-Sama's ears, woe betide the whole race of European vipers, who have been too long spared by an over-merciful monarch."

"Matthias must be sent for," said the Father Commissary when Faxegava had departed; "yet I would fain have avoided this necessity. If our own lives were at stake, nothing would have induced me to recall him; but the number of the prisoners must be made up, and if he does not appear to-morrow we shall risk the lives of many without saving him. Would to God that I had two lives to lay down instead of one."

The words did not fall unheeded on the ears of a young man who was standing at that moment by the side of Father Baptiste. An earnest whisper reached the superior's ear—"Do not send for him to-day, father; if needs be I will fetch him myself early to-morrow."

The priest turned round and looked with surprise at the speaker. "It is well, my son," he said; "I leave the matter in your hands."

"But will you then sign this paper, father, and trust me with it?"

Father Baptiste saw these words hastily written on a sheet of paper, "I command you, in virtue of holy obedience, not to return to Meaco without an order from the superior." Father Baptiste started, and once more looked inquiringly at Isafai (for it was with him that he was speaking). "My son," he said, "I must know what is your meaning?"

"Oh, father, you can trust me. Matthias will appear to-morrow, and the number of the prisoners will be complete; not one will be missing. Trust me, father; but for God's sake sign this paper."

"I dare not," exclaimed Father Baptiste with some agitation; "I cannot sanction—"

The young catechist looked almost sternly at the venerable priest. "Do you mistrust me, father?"

"You have no right to dispose of a life—"

"Father, put on your stole, and come into the confessional; *there* you will not tell me that I have no right to do for a weak brother what Christ has done for us all."

When Isafai rose from his knees and left the church he held in his hands the paper signed by Father Baptiste.

CHAPTER XII.

THE TWO MATTHIASES.

Matthew, the blind pedlar, was standing at the door of Agatha's house on the following morning watching for the first sounds of life within its walls, and longing for the moment when he could speak with Laurentia, who had been residing with Andrew Ongasamara's family from the time that her brother had entered the Franciscan Convent. She had been in a fearful state of anxiety since the last troubles had began. At the time when all the women of that household had been engaged in preparing their dresses for the day of martyrdom, she alone had appeared sad and depressed; a nervous restlessness was visible in all her movements, and Isafai's encouraging words seemed to bring neither courage nor peace to her heart. Her friends concluded that the hopes of earthly happiness, which had occupied her mind since his return and his conversion, had attached her so much to this mortal life that her spirit was shrinking from the prospect of suffering and death. When Agatha spoke to her once in this sense, she had answered somewhat impatiently, and did not seem inclined to disclose her thoughts. When the news came that it was only twenty-five persons whose names had been taken down at the time when guards had been set to the convent of the Porziuncula who were condemned to death, she turned pale, and was seized with a violent trembling. This had happened the day after her meeting with her brother on his way to the village, where the Father Commissary had sent him to catechize in preparation for the arrival of a priest. She had sought the next day in every direction for old Matthew, and had remained awake all night watching for his footsteps and longing for his arrival. At last she rose, looked out of the window, and saw the old sightless man patiently leaning against the garden walls, with his beads in his hands, the first rays of the sun shining on his pale face and his grey hair; she hastened to fetch him into the house.

"My dear maiden," he kindly said, "I have obeyed your summons, and if there is anything that old Matthew can do to help or console you, he is, you know, at your service. And so your brother Matthias is one of that glorious number who are about to suffer for Christ's sake. There are many, many fervent souls in this city that envy his fate. Take courage then, and rejoice that one so dear to you is destined to win the palm of martyrdom."

"Has he been sent for?" Laurentia asked in a low voice.

"Late last night I put that question to the Father Commissary, and he said that your betrothed, that Isafai had undertaken to fetch him from Taima."

"Oh no! Oh, my God, do not tell me so!" exclaimed Laurentia, wringing her hands. "Oh, Matthew, seek him; seek Isafai, bring him to me. He must not go on this errand; he is not gone yet? Oh, say he is not!"

"I know he carried away with him last night an order from the Father Commissary, and went in the direction of Taima."

"Then all is lost."

"Laurentia, is it possible that you have ceased to think and to feel that there is no joy and no honor like that of dying for the faith? Would you not be ready yourself to lay down your life for Christ? Were they, then, vain boastings, those words I heard you utter not a year ago when I rebuked you for rashly rushing into danger, and you said, 'The worst that can happen to me is to die'?"

"There are far worse miseries, Matthew, than to die; I feel that still. Is Isafai indeed gone? Are you sure that he went? Why did he not come to me first? Oh, you all are cruel, very cruel. God help me, I almost abhor now that Japanese courage which you once reproached me for idolizing. Was it necessary to send for him?"

"The number of prisoners must be complete. The executions answer to the list which the Kumbo-Sama has signed. Matthias could not have escaped his doom, my poor child; and his absence would have put in peril all the Christians of this place."

"The number must be complete!" murmured

Laurentia. "But you say there are so many longing to die in this city."

"Would you rob your brother of his crown?"

"Oh, talk not to me of crowns; talk not of palms; you drive me wild, Matthew; you torture me—"

"Laurentia! Laurentia! Have you lost your faith?"

"Lost my faith! Oh, Matthew, if I had lost my faith I should not suffer as I now do; it is because I believe that my heart is breaking."

"My poor child, speak; what do you mean? what do you fear?"

"Did I say I feared? Why do you take up my words so strangely? Where is Andrew? Who will help me? who will counsel me? I must go to the church and pray. There only can this suspense be endured. Agatha, come to me."

When her adopted mother appeared, Laurentia flung herself into her arms and sobbed on her breast; but she did not meet with the sympathy which her aching heart needed. Agatha was kind, but she felt disappointed in Laurentia. Her heroism of character led her to wonder at what seemed a want of faith in her friend. She would have expected her to greet with congratulations a brother about to die for his religion, to have followed him to the cross with blessings, and encouraged him by words and by looks to suffer bravely, and to die with exultation.

Matthew was silently praying for the weeping

maiden, but grieving also at her uncontrolled agitation, at her wild and incoherent expressions. A horseman stopped at the gate, and they held their breath in suspense. It lasted but a moment —that terrible suspense. Isafai sprung to the ground and hurried to Laurentia's side. She hid her face in her hands, and cried, "Have you brought him with you?"

He removed her hands from her face. He compelled her to raise her eyes to his. He gazed upon her with a look of tender affection. "Laurentia, I must speak with you alone," he said; "you are my betrothed. I have things to say to you which others must not hear—come to that garden seat where we used to sit when we were children."

Agatha looked anxiously at them both. There was something peculiar in the manner of those affianced lovers—something almost joyous in his countenance, but a solemnity in it also. From the moment he had arrived Laurentia seemed to have grown calm.

They sat down side by side, and when they were alone, she said, "Where is he?"

"At Taima, dearest."

"Is he coming?"

"No: I have carried to him an order from Father Baptiste, not to return to Meaco without permission."

"Thank God! thank God!" she ejaculated.

"Yes: thank God, my Laurentia; thank God that it is so."

"*You* do not know," she exclaimed, passionately clasping her hands, "what a blessing it is. Oh, Isafai, how did it come to pass? Old Matthew told me that all on that list must die."

"*All* named in that list *must* die."

"What do you mean? I thought you said— Do not mock my anguish. Is he come? Is he coming? How is he? Is his step firm? Is his eye bright? Does he look like one who is about to die with—Oh, Isafai, speak!" and she threw herself on her knees at his feet. "He does not, tell me he does not, look like an apostate!"

"He is one of those," he answered, gently raising her, "to whom God shows great mercy; whose spirit is willing, but whose flesh is weak."

"Then, if he is weak he will perish!" she wildly exclaimed.

"He is safe. Have I not told you that he runs no danger?"

"But the list, the list—his name is on the list."

"Have you forgotten that his name is *mine?*"

Oh, what a cry that was that burst from those white lips, and with what a glazed eye and livid cheek the maiden stood as one transfixed, gazing on that noble face and form as if it had turned into some fearful vision scaring her soul with terror.

"Laurentia," he began.

"Do not speak to me," she cried; "do not say those words again. Oh, Matthias! Matthias! fatal name! it must not be—it shall not be!"

"Laurentia, my beloved, I have loved you truly and long, in the darkness of unbelief, in the full light of truth, in absence and in sorrow, in hope and in joy; but never has my heart throbbed with such intense happiness, such exulting joy in our happiest hours as it does this day. Do not look at me sadly or wildly, my beloved. It is no time for tears; it is a brighter day than a bridal one; a deeper bliss than earth can give. I have loved you, my own Laurentia, far, far more than myself, but far less than Jesus. It was, indeed, a day of misery when I took leave of you five years ago, without faith in God, without hope for the future; but to-day I go to Him through the only sure road, the only secure way."

"And you leave a woman's broken heart behind."

"God will heal it; God will raise it; God will cherish it. I have prayed for you, I have prayed for myself. Laurentia, this is the answer."

"You have been heard," she cried; "but did you ask this for me; that I should see you die (and die for me, for my brother,) and live on in this world which you so joyfully leave?—Oh, Isafai!"

"Do you grudge me my happiness?"

"Do you dare to talk of happiness to me?"

"Are you not a Christian? Come, Laurentia, let me not bear away with me to the heaven which I trust so soon to reach, the remembrances of your reproaches, of your grief. Lift up your heart.— Dry your eyes. Tears must not stain the bright robe of martyrdom—it is crimson drops, not a woman's tears that must bedew it. Call to mind what has never passed your lips; the agony of that day when your brother fell."

"But when you have died for him who knows—"

"Do not fear. There is an hour when a man's prayer is all powerful with God. He grants the request of those who die for Him; and when the spear has pierced my heart, grace and strength will be given to Matthias. Even now our blessed Lord hears me; even now the ardent desire of my soul is accomplished. I see it; I feel it. Strength has come to you, my Laurentia; the colour has returned to your cheek, the light to your eye. You will rejoice, even now, for me and with me, that I can die this day for my brother and for my faith. Does it not all come back to you: the thoughts of that glory we have so often spoken of; of those immortal hopes we have shared; of that Sacred Heart we adore?"

"Isafai," she murmured, and then in a firmer voice went on, "I will not offer to God a grudging sacrifice. I have been weak and blind, and earthly passion had caused for a moment the realities of faith to disappear from my sight; but *now* I can soar with you, my beloved, above this world's hopes and fears. I feel the spirit which was once mine kindling anew in my heart. Yes, I can kneel and bless you, and thank you, Isafai, that you are going to die for my brother. I know you will not die in vain. A martyr's blood has often purchased back for Christ an apostate, won back a soul from the threshold of hell. Will it not win courage and strength for a willing heart? No, I no longer am afraid of my own feelings. For one instant—yes at your feet I will confess it—for one instant I felt as if I should hate my brother if you died for him, but this fear has passed away never to return. I have thought of her who stood at the foot of the Cross where Jesus was dying for us, and who felt in her heart an immense, boundless love for those He was buying at so dear a price; and that thought has stilled for ever the wild impulses of a selfish agony."

"Will you come with me to the convent, my beloved? Will you accompany me as far as may be on that path I long to tread?"

Laurentia turned as pale as death, but lifting up her eyes to heaven, she steadily gazed a moment on the sky, as if to gather strength from its blue depths, and then exclaimed, "Yes, to the convent first and then to the cross. This is a strange bridal day. We were to have been married this month. Now nothing can part us for eternity.— You have linked my soul to yours by a tie that can never be riven. Lead the way, Isafai, and do not fear that I shall faint on the road."

With blessings and with tears the family of Andrew gathered around the betrothed and accompanied them to the convent. They looked with admiration and envy on the young hero; and with more sympathy than pity on his bride. They were boldly consistent these Japanese Christians, and congratulated their martyrs on the approach of death. They did not understand how it could be sad to suffer a few hours, and triumph for ever; to part for a while, and be united in eternity. They *had* faith.

Meantime Grace Ucondono had heard that every person in the Franciscan convent was condemned to death, and that the very children there were refusing to receive liberty and life at the price of their religion. She thought at first that little Augustine was not included in the number, but when told that the child had hurried there on the first news of the condemnation of the Spanish fathers, and that his name was in the list drawn up at their house, she became most anxious to see him, and to let his mother know of his danger. She could only get there a short time before the hour appointed for the departure of the prisoners from Meaco. The convent presented an extraordinary appearance. It was almost impossible to approach it through the crowds that were now fast gathering from all directions. The heathens as well as the Christians were flocking from all parts to witness this singular spectacle. It seemed a religious ceremony far more than a preparation for execution. There was sorrow in many faces, but more so in those of the heathens than the Christians. These were filled with a holy exultation which seemed to raise them above themselves.— Grace and her father Justo made their way at last to the inside of the court in which stood the convent, and begged to see the boy Augustine.

"Ah, lady!" he exclaimed when he caught sight of Grace, "you are come to wish me joy, I suppose. I told you I was on the list, and now the happy day is come. Have you heard that Isafai has played a trick to Matthias? Poor Matthias is away in the mountains catechising, and that cunning Isafai, whose name is also Matthias, has taken his place and cheated him of his rights. Don't you think, lady, it is very hard on poor Matthias?"

"Isafai!" exclaimed Grace with agitation, "Laurentia's betrothed!"

"Laurentia is here," said the child; "they came together an hour ago, and they are praying in the Church. Father Baptiste and our brother Paul have been preaching so beautifully about martyrdom. Oh, how very good God is to let a little child like me be a martyr: it is, I am sure, Father Francis's doing; he did not give me back my eyes for nothing."

"Then, my boy," said Grace, embracing him, "I suppose you would not be willing, even if it was possible, to come away with me and save your life?"

"No, lady," said the child with a bright smile. "I had rather die for Jesus Christ than live with you, though you look very good and are very beautiful."

"If you were a king's son would you not wish to return to your father's Court?"

"I am going to my Father's Court in Heaven; I don't want to hear about any other."

"My little child," said Grace, looking upon the boy with a kind of respectful awe, "I have something to say to you from that lady I told you of."

"Ah !" said the child, "I have often thought of what you said about her ; she was to send me a° I think."

"She has offered up for you a more painful cross than the one you will find, my child, prepared for you at Nangazaqui,—she is your mother, and she is the wife of the King of Arima. She might have told him, and he would have sent armies of soldiers to get possession of his son ; but, Augustine, he is a heathen, and she would not claim you from your Christian fathers, though her heart was yearning to save you."

"To *save* me, lady ! Did you not say my mother was a Christian ?"

"Thank God she is."

"Then she must be glad that I go to heaven; and she will come there soon herself—tell her I shall be looking out for her. Grace,—is not that your name?—I should like to send my mother something." The boy thought a moment, then he said, "Come to the high tower, where we are going first, and try to get as near as you can to the cart when it moves away ! I think I shall then have something to give you for my mother."

"I will endeavour to do so," said Grace ; and then, her heart being to full to converse an longer,

*18

she went into the chapel, which was decorated with flowers and brilliantly lit. Father Baptiste, that true religious, that "worthy captain of a glorious troop," as the Jesuit historian calls him, was saying a last prayer before the altar (lately raised to the seraphic saint of Assisi,) and asking his blessing on his children, and then turning towards the crowd within and without the church, he raised his hands, and pronounced a few parting words, which remained forever stamped in the hearts of his hearers.

The hour had come; the guards who were to conduct the prisoners first to the place of execution in the town and then to Nangazaqui, were arrived. The carts were waiting at the door of the convent; one by one the victims took their places. Father Baptiste was the last. He held the child Augustine in his arms.

One of the chief bonzes, who had come to feast his eyes with the sufferings of the Christians, cried out to the boy, "Come to me, Augustine; I can save thy life and make thy fortune."

"Will you let me be a Christian, and save the fathers also?"

"No, I speak to you alone. Do not you know what they are going to do with you?"

"Yes," cried the boy with intrepidity, "they are going to tie our hands behind our backs and to cut off our ears, and then they will take us to Nangazaqui and crucify us there. I had rather die with the fathers than live a heathen."

The carts moved slowly along the streets, towards the place where the first part of the sentence was to be executed. Then it became apparent that it was not through ignorance of their approaching fate that the three little martyrs had been so bold in word and in action. They bore, without a groan, the cruel treatment which was inflicted upon them as well as on the other prisoners; and as they left Meaco, and even whilst the blood was streaming down their innocent faces, they were the first to intone the psalm "Laudate Pueri Dominum."

Grace, who with her father, and Andrew, and Agatha, and a great number of Christians, was pressing as near as possible to the cart to catch the accents of that glorious chant, found herself close to the little Augustine. He caught sight of her, and eagerly stretching out his hand, which he had disengaged from the cords, he put something into hers.

"Take this to my mother," he whispered, "and tell her that it hurt me very much when they cut off the tips of my ears; but I did not cry because I am a martyr, and I send her this bit of my flesh to put her in mind of the sufferings which her little son has endured for Christ's sake. Perhaps she will show it to my heathen father, and in heaven I will pray for them both."

This and other relics of the same kind were bedewed with tears, and, as in the days of the early Church, carried away by the Christians with tender and affectionate devotion. When Father Organtin, who with his priests had been commanded by the authorities to remain within the walls of the college, received those first tokens of his children's and his brethren's sufferings, he lifted up his voice like Hezekiah and wept aloud. "Behold," he exclaimed, "Behold, my Divine Saviour, the first-fruits of the present persecution! Grant that the blood which waters the earth may bring forth many saints to praise thy holy name by their lives and by their deaths."

CHAPTER XIII.

MARTYRDOM.

THE signal for departure had been given, and the long pilgrimage of suffering, the "Via dolorosa," of that heroic band was begun. The cart slowly passed through the towns, the villages, and the plains of the Ximo, through Ozaca and Saccai on to Nangazaqui, the Christian city.

Many Christians at Meaco implored to share the fate of the prisoners, but Fazambura, the brother of the Governor of Nangazaqui, who had been entrusted with the execution of the Emperor's orders, had given positive directions that this singular favour should be universally refused, and would not even allow the relations and friends to accompany them in the carts, or to ride by their side, so numbers followed them on foot, with tears, with prayers, and with hymns of praise. After a while the Christians of Meaco fell off from the cortege, and others took their places. From each town as they passed, men, women, and children joined that extraordinary procession, every day newly escorted by fresh gathering crowds. But there was one pilgrim who never wearied, who never retraced her steps, whose strength seemed supernatural; whose eyes were ever fixed on one of the carts, and the tones of whose melodious voice were heard pouring forth its thrilling notes of praise at morning dawn and at the sunset hour, leading the choir of that triumphant march, and marshalling the weeping crowds on the road of sorrow, whilst she never shed a tear herself. This was Laurentia, the bride and the sister of the two Matthiases. She begged of the Christians, in each place through which they passed, clothes (for it was fearfully cold) and food for the prisoners. She ministered unceasingly to their wants. The heathens watched with amazement that pale delicate woman, who looked more like an attendant spirit than a being of flesh and blood, as she hovered around the carts and spoke words of encouragement to each of its occupants in turn, reminding them of their high hopes and of the blessed heaven in view. She had herself surrendered all thought, all cares but one—life had no longer any meaning for her, but in the reflected light of eternity.

At Ozaca a pilgrim joined the escort who never spoke to any one, who walked alone, apart from the rest, whose face was concealed, but who also rendered every possible service to the captives, and never handed anything to them but on his knees. His voice never was heard but when the psalm Miserere was sung; then it rose with a mournful and sweet power, like the wail of the wind at night in the halls of a deserted house.

At Saccai the Christians were deeply moved,

and, at the sight of their mutilated and bleeding brethren, on the point of rising in insurrection.— Then the proclamation which was carried at the head of the procession was changed, and the profession of Christianity, which in the first had not been denounced, was now declared to be high treason to the State.

Laurentia was arrested and accused of being a Christian. Then the pale cheek glowed with joy; the eye, sunken with fatigue, gleamed with a new brightness; the step, which was beginning to falter grew more bold and more firm; and with an unspeakable expression of faith and of hope she spoke words like those of Esau when pleading for his birthright, "Bless me also, O my God! Hast thou not a cross for me also, O my Father?"

She was numbered with the prisoners; that blessing was granted to her. And then the companion of her labours, whose face she had never beheld, was also brought forward and charged likewise "with having been with these men from the beginning." She raised her eyes to see who was this new comrade in suffering and in glory. He was bound and standing by the side of Philip the Mexican. She thought for a moment that she was dreaming. No, it was him—it was her brother! But how changed! Not a trace of colour on his marble cheek, but it was not the paleness of fear that had blanched them; not a black hair on his young head; a night had done the work of years, and he stood before her grey-headed in youth, and bent like a man bowed down with a heavy burden.

Did wild thoughts pass through her mind? Did she cast one passionate glance back at the past?—Did the tide of earthly love and earthly yearnings turn once again in that hour? No; the sacrifice had been complete; the surrender entire. No other cry burst from her lips than a fervent "Deo gratias." She never feared, she never doubted; she trusted God and she trusted her brother. Their eyes had met. The reward had been given. The prayer of one about to die had been heard—onward they went, onward on their way to glory and to death.

When the holy band arrived at Omura an aged man was there, who after many efforts and struggles succeeded in approaching them. This was Father Rodriguez, the Emperor's interpreter.

The Rector of the College at Nangazaqui had received the following touching letter from Father Baptiste:—

"We set out from Meaco four-and-twenty in company, all of us condemned to be crucified at Nangazaqui. Three religious of the Society of Jesus, six of the order of St. Francis, the rest Japanese and catechists. We are all content to die for the faith. I beg, in the name of all the prisoners, that your reverence will use your interest with the judges in order that we may have leave to receive the sacraments and the Bishop's blessing before we suffer; and we could wish to see all your fathers there at the same time, to whose prayers we heartily commend ourselves."

No sooner had the Rector communicated this letter to the Provincial than they resolved to send Father Rodriguez and another father with him to Omura, where the prisoners were to arrive the following day, and there, if possible, to say Mass and give them Communion on their way. But Fazambura, the only person with authority sufficient to have given permission for this departure from the usual order of proceedings, had gone on to Nangazaqui by a different road, and this consolation was not vouchsafed to them. It was with the greatest difficulty that Father Rodriguez obtained leave from the guards to speak with the prisoners. But at last, by dint of prayers and efforts, he succeeded, and with outstretched arms and streaming eyes he drew near to that holy company who were about to die, as he had so longed himself to die. No sooner did Father Baptiste see him than he fell on his knees and cried out, "Father Rodriguez, I and my brethren implore the pardon of the fathers of your holy society for the trouble we have given you since our arrival in Japan. We are now about to yield up our lives for our common mother the Church, and we crave, as dying men, your pardon and your blessing."

Father Rodriguez had also fallen on his knees, and would not assume any other posture till he had compelled Father Baptiste to rise. Then from the fulness of his heart he poured forth the tenderest expressions of love and of admiration.

"There is nothing to forgive," he cried; "speak

not of pardon, O blessed martyrs of Christ, or else, in the name of the Society, let me crave yours for what we may have done to grieve you. O venerable father! O holy and blessed brethren! God be with you in this hour of suffering and of triumph. Pray for us whom you leave behind, unworthy to follow you, unworthy to share your glory and to walk by your side."

Then turning to Paul Michi, to James Kisai, and John Gotto, the three Jesuit brothers, and to the little child Augustine, who had grown up amongst them as a flower in a forest of pines, he fell on their necks, and wept over them in speechless emotion, even as the early Christians when parting with St. Paul.

The town of Nangazaqui was in an extraordinary state of agitation. The Christians from the whole of the neighboring country were crowding to the scene where the great tragedy was to take place, and Fazambura became alarmed at the excitement which was beginning to disturb the public mind. He had promised Paul Michi, for whom he had an ancient friendship, to lodge all the prisoners in the town for one night, previous to the execution, and to allow them the happiness of conferring with the priests at Nangazaqui, of hearing Mass and going to communion; but he now retracted all these concessions. He was frightened at the power exercised by those chained, suffering, and doomed men. The bonzes had gathered around him, and reproached him bitterly for the means the Emperor was taking of spreading, they said, rather than annihilating the Christian religion. "Strange method," they exclaimed, "of discrediting this foreign worship, to carry about the country those men who smile at sufferings, and glory in disgrace. The enchanted tongue of that Paul Michi, who never opens his mouth but he makes converts; the eloquence of that Father Baptiste of the Ascension (as they call him, and well they may, for he seems ever in a kind of ecstacy, half way between earth and heaven,) are seducing on the road as many persons, as can get to speak with them. Another such exhibition, a dozen more such martyrs, and we may as well shut up the temples, and call the King of Spain to reign over us. We will let the Emperor know that there is no one, however high in office or position, who can withstand the influence of Paul Michi's arguments." This was said in so pointed a manner that Fazambura grew deeply alarmed, and commanded that fifty crosses should be erected on a hill outside the walls of Nangazaqui, and hurried on the preparations for the execution as much as he could; but he sent a private message to Father Rodriguez, that at the hermitage of St. Lazarus he might meet his brethren once more and administer to them spiritual consolation.

In that little wayside chapel, which Isafai with the aid of Mancia Ito had erected on his return from Europe, and which he had thought of enlarging one day and dedicating to Mary, Star of the

Sea, the procession halted. Fair was the view of sea and land from that promontory. It was a bright cold day; bright as the martyrs' hopes, and cold as the grave that was preparing for them.— Father Rodriguez confessed the Jesuit brothers, and received the vows of those who had not yet been finally admitted into the society. Every one of the band of martyrs approached the tribunal of penance in that solemn hour; and when they came out of the chapel, and the word was given, and the march was resumed, Fazambura marvelled at the joy and peace which was beaming in their faces. He expressed his surprise to Father Rodriguez, who eagerly embraced the opportunity of explaining to him the sublime truths of the Christian faith.

The man of the world listened to him with attention. "It is very fine," he said; "perhaps it may be true; but to die on a cross would not at all suit me."

The father took occasion to entreat that the two prisoners who had been made on the road should be released. He pleaded that they were not included in the original list, and that it must be contrary to the Emperor's will that they should be executed with the rest. "I have taken his Majesty's pleasure on the subject," was the answer. "The case is a peculiar one. The man was appointed painter in her Majesty's household, and left it to dwell amongst men who have proved traitors and foreign enemies. He needs must die. As to that pale, dark-eyed sister of his, who was nearly swallowed up by the earthquake at Fuximi, and who was also at one time in great favour with the Empress, she is not to die, but an order has been sent for her banishment to the Island of Cozuxima, where she may worship as she pleases with the sea fowl and the wild fishermen who alone dwell there."

And now the long pilgrimage was drawing to a close. The crosses had been erected on a height, which became afterwards so often the scene of the death of Christians that it received the name of Calvary, or the Mount of Martyrs. When the procession halted, and the prisoners had descended from the carts, the boldest of the spectators held their breath in silent awe, pity, and admiration. Augustine and his two young companions discovered instantly that there were three crosses smaller than the rest, and they ran up and took possession of them with a joy which deeply affected even the heathen Governor. Anthony's parents, who inhabited Nangazaqui, hastened to the boy's side, and though they were Christians, they pleaded with their child that he was too young to be a martyr. He would never reply but by asking if he was "too young to go to heaven—too young to save his soul?" Others were encouraged by their friends to bear bravely the sufferings of a moment, and so to win an eternal crown. One young man, when his father addressed him in this strain, kissed his rosary and held it out to him as the last token of his love and of his faith. The priests, the men, and the children were bound each to his cross, not nailed to it as their Lord—theirs was not to be the lingering torture of the three hours' agony; but the spear was to pierce their hearts even as His was pierced for their sake. There were some short and tender partings, hurried blessings, murmured prayers. Father Rodriguez and his companion Father Passius went from one to another of the martyrs, suggesting thoughts of heavenly comfort and divine consolation. Then a deep silence followed, only now and then broken by the words, "Jesus, Mary," uttered with intense feeling. The signal was about to be given, but ere it was made, Father Baptiste was heard intoning in a loud voice the canticle of Zacharias, "Benedictus dominus Deus Israel." The other martyrs joined in it; the shrill voices of the children swelled the triumphant chant, and a woman bore her part in that dying melody; but before the psalm was ended the ground was deluged with blood; and twenty-five martyrs had given up their souls to God.

A cry of anguish and of triumph burst from the crowd of Christians, who could no longer be restrained. They rushed to the crosses; they knelt at their feet; they gathered up the blood; they carried off the clothes of the martyrs—many were praying aloud, weeping, or gazing in silence on those beautiful corpses hanging serenely between heaven and earth, some with the eyes modestly bent down, and others looking up to heaven as if fixed in some wonderful ecstasy. Father Rodriguez went up to Laurentia, who was sitting between two crosses like that blessed one, the thought of whom had supported her through her long martyrdom of the heart. She had stood till the end came; when all was over she sank down on the ground, and remained there as silent and as motionless as the bodies of the saints around her. It was an extraordinary scene, a wonderful subject of thought, that so many human souls, widely differing in all but their faith, should have arrived at the same glorious end. The Spanish Franciscan priest and his companions, medicant friars, born under other skies, come from the far-off realms of the Western continent to evangelize this remote island in the East; and amongst them, wearing the same dress, living now under the same rule, that poor prodigal from the shores of the New World, Philip the Mexican, driven from his native land by the contempt of his countrymen and the indignation of his parents, and drifted from shore to shore by the billows of a merciful ocean into the port where angels were in wait for him. Japanese youths, born amidst the idols of a false religion, and at last clad in the armour of the ascetic army of St. Ignatius; children on the threshold of life; men in the full strength of manhood; the aged on the verge of the grave. Those noble warriors of the Cross, those champions of Christ's army, those heroes of the Church.— "Let them rest in peace." We need not speak of them here; they do not need our idle praise, for they are raised on our altars, and every year we say from our hearts on the anniversary day of their death, "Pray for us, O holy martyrs of Japan."

And now what was the fate of those who remained behind? Where is Laurentia, the widowed bride, the bereaved sister? What has become of her? She is banished to a wild island of the ocean, where she is henceforward to dwell, copying the example of her who languished fifteen years in this cold world after the light had set for her, not amidst the darkness of Calvary, or the sepulchre, but on the heights of Mount Olivet. The imperial guards have carried her thither, and left her there on the day which followed the execution of the martyrs. A great number of Christians accompanied her to the shore; her old friend, Matthew the comb-seller was there, and Anselm the apostolic stroller.— Both had made their way to Nangazaqui in the hope of being included in the noble army of martyrs who had just won their crowns; but long as they had worked in the burthen and heat of the day, the hour of rest had not yet rung for them: yet a little while they had to tarry and carry the cross on which they had so longed to stretch their weary limbs. As the maiden passed them and heard their murmured blessings, she was seen to weep. "Dear friends," she said, as she entered the boat and they were bidding her farewell, "I weep not for my blessed ones, but for myself, because the hope of dying for Christ is now taken from me."

"Take courage, my child," replied Matthew; "the Church honors the confessorship of long and painful suffering equally with the triumphs of the martyrs." It was his own consolation.

Laurentia spent the remainder of her life in the Island of Cozuxima; the only companions of her solitude seven or eight poor fishermen, who, out of their scanty provisions, gave her enough to sustain existence. It was but little she needed; and in the words of a letter to Father Organtin, "she felt richer upon that ocean rock than she had ever done in her days of youthful joy and hope, and could ill have brooked to live elsewhere." Cozuxima was to her what the cave near Marseilles was to St. Mary Magdalen, what her cell is to the true Carmelite nun. In its forlorn solitude God was pleased to pour into her soul an abundance of spiritual consolations. She heard in spirit every Mass that was offered in the wide world. In her eyes the barren rock was Mount Calvary. The only treasures she coveted—an abridgment of the Scriptures, "The Lives of the Saints," an hour-glass to regulate the time of her meditations, two lights, a little bell, and a picture of a priest saying Mass. Her life was one incessant contemplation. In the fissures of the cliff she saw the cave of Bethlehem; in the fisherman's boat the bark in which Jesus sat; in every tree a cross; and in the moanings of the wind at night, or the voice of the great deep, she heard the cry of the "Miserere" and the hymn "De profundis."

Grace Ucondono came once to see her in that solitude. They sat on the wild sea-coast as they had once sat under the shade of the pink blossoming almon trees of the palace at Meaco. The scene was changed, so were their lives. The two brides of Japan had found their vocation—one, in the hour in which she had been the minister of a great spiritual gift to the soul of her friend; the other, when at the foot of the cross she had received a second baptism of blood. The one, had been called to active work in courts and in hovels; she had a restless love of souls, which found its vent in action; he whom she had once loved with a human affection was treading in the steps of the successors of St. Francis Xavier, and fighting the battle of the Cross with every weapon which intellect, and talent, and energy, as well as divine grace can furnish, and she rejoiced in the thought. The other, had been carried to the very gates of heaven, and seen her beloved ones pass through those bright portals before; and had remained transfixed in contemplation of that celestial vision. Her struggles were spiritual ones, her weapons were prayers; she pleaded; she suffered; she worshipped. St. Theresa was her model, and the little barren isle of the ocean her Mount Carmel. Both these Christian maidens were blessed, both lived wholly detached from earthly ties; and it was well for them that it was so. It was not a time to marry and to give in marriage, as Paul Sacondono had said. There were fierce breakers ahead, and dark were the storms that threatened the Church of Japan.

The children of the Christians who married in

www.ingramcontent.com/pod-product-compliance
Lightning Source LLC
Chambersburg PA
CBHW031819230426
43669CB00009B/1197